KS3 Science

Homework Book 2

Collins

D1461719

Graham Farrall

William Collins's dream of knowledge for all began with the publication of his first book in 1819. A self-educated mill worker, he not only enriched millions of lives, but also founded a flourishing publishing house. Today, staying true to this spirit, Collins books are packed with inspiration, innovation and practical expertise. They place you at the centre of a world of possibility and give you exactly what you need to explore it.

Collins. Freedom to teach.
Published by Collins
An imprint of HarperCollinsPublishers
77-85 Fulham Palace Road
Hammersmith
London
W6 8JB

Browse the complete Collins catalogue at
www.collinseducation.com

Commissioned by Penny Fowler
Project management by Alexandra Riley
Edited by Anita Clark
Proof read by Camilla Behrens
Original concept design by Jordan Publishing Design
Page layout and cover design by eMC Design Ltd, www.emcdesign.org.uk
Illustrations by Jerry Fowler

Production by Leonie Kellman

Printed and bound by Printing Express, Hong Kong

Contents

Introduction

Welcome to Collins KS3 Science!

Exciting homework for every Pupil Book spread

The Homework Book contains three exciting and levelled activities for every spread in the Pupil Book. There are three styles of question – test yourself, creative and digital – so that learning science is engaging and fun.

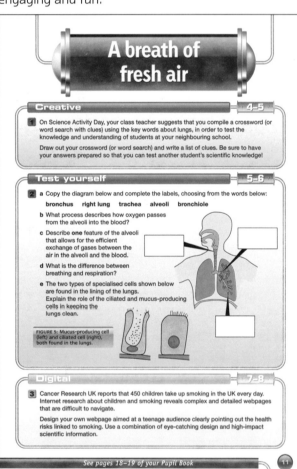

Test yourself

Test your knowledge of a topic with comprehensive test yourself questions. At the back of the book you are able to check your answers or, if you don't want to, you can tear them out at the start of your course. These questions will give you extra practice, helping you to succeed in school tests at KS3 and to prepare for GCSE.

Creative

Do you want to be a journalist for a day? How about running an advertising campaign? Or how about designing a colourful poster for your classroom?

With creative questions you can really put your science knowledge to the test with a full range of engaging activities making science fun.

Digital

Put your scientific skills to the test with our digital homeworks covering everything from creating PowerPoint presentations to making podcasts and writing wikis to share with your entire class.

If you need help on how to make a podcast or how to set up a wiki there is advice for students and teachers on our website www.collinseducation.com/ks3science

How Science Works

Look out for our HSW icons throughout the Homework Book. This is where you will really show How Science Works in your homework.

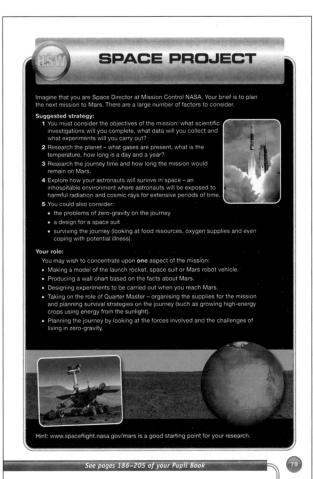

Mid-Topic Projects

About half way through the topic you get a chance to see how much you've learned already by working on a project in groups in class and also at home. Science is put into context as you learn how science relates to the everyday world and has an impact on us all.

Free teaching notes for every mid-topic project are available at www.collinseducation.com/ks3science

Record your progress

At the back of this book you will see your student progress cards. All of the homeworks are levelled into levels 4–5, 5–6 and 7–8. As you work through the book, mark which homeworks you are completing for each lesson. As you move through your Key Stage 3 course you will be able to track your progress throughout each topic.

Student Progress Card	Name:		
Organisms, Behaviour and Health	4-5	5-6	7-8
Keeping Healthy			
A balanced diet			
Is my diet OK?			
Eating food			
Do I have enough energy?			
A breath of fresh air			
A healthy heart			
Measuring your pulse			
How do you know if you are fit?			
Studying Disease			
History of disease			
The infection cycle			
Preventing disease			
Sexually transmitted diseases			

A balanced diet

1 Imagine that you are a food scientist giving advice to children about healthy eating. You decide to make a model of a plate of food to illustrate your talk. Your model must be labelled with information about the different types of food along with explanations about the meal and how the body uses the nutrition gained from it.

(Hint: www.eatwell.gov.uk is a great website to get you started. You will find it very useful throughout this topic.)

Test yourself 5–6

2

Food	Energy per 100g of food (kJ)	Nutrients per 100g of each food			
		Protein (g)	Fat (g)	Carbohydrate (g)	Salt (g)
Cheese spread	606	8.0	10.5	4.0	1.0
Baked beans	300	4.9	0.2	12.9	0.8
Olive oil spread	2203	0.2	59.0	1.0	0.8
Yoghurt	283	4.8	0.1	8.3	0.2

a Which of the **three** nutrients in the baked beans provides the most energy?

b Which food would lead to the highest rise in blood pressure if eaten in excess?

c Which of the nutrients is needed for growth and repair?

d Why do manufacturers always display the nutrient content per 100g?

e A worker's daily energy intake is 12000 kJ. What percentage of this intake would be supplied by 200g of baked beans?

Digital 7–8

3 Supermarkets make a high proportion of their profit from ready-prepared meals which can be high in fats, sugar, salt and flavourings.

a Research online the nutritional content of ready-prepared meals.

b Write an extended essay on the ethics of making a profit in such a way when the supermarkets should be more responsible and act as guardians for our health.

FIGURE 1: Ready-prepared meals can have a low nutritional value.

See pages 8–9 of your Pupil Book

Is my diet OK?

4-5

Creative

1 The government is concerned about the future health of the nation.

Imagine that you have been asked to write a TV script for a government health campaign that will advise the public of the benefits of eating five pieces of fruit and vegetables a day. Next lesson you may be selected to read out your script so make your work exciting, memorable and scientific – you may even wish to use your packed lunch to help as a prompt!

FIGURE 2: Fruit and vegetables are essential in a healthy diet.

Test yourself

5-6

2 a Complete the following sentences by making **one** selection from each column.

Vitamins and minerals	**can be**	the risk of cancers.
Too much salt	**responsible for**	increasing blood pressure.
Fish oils rich in omega-3		obesity.
Too much carbohydrate		the risk of heart disease.
Too little fibre in a diet	**can reduce**	swelling of the feet.
Too much salt		bowel cancer.

b Which organ is responsible for the removal of salt from the body?

c It is important that athletes maintain a balanced diet but why would an athlete need to increase the quantity of food eaten when training?

d If you eat your evening meal at 6.00 p.m., skip breakfast the following morning and then eat your next main meal at 12.00 noon, how many hours will it be before your body replenishes its energy resources?

e Using the information from part **d**, explain why you will feel tired and lacking in energy if you skip breakfast.

f Why is it recommended that a balanced diet should include oily fish?

Digital

7-8

3 In 1795, British sailors gained the nickname 'limey' when limes were carried on board sailing ships embarking on long sea journeys. The limes prevented the men from dying from scurvy.

a Research online the history behind the word 'limey'.

b Produce a scientific cartoon strip (taking pictures from the Internet) telling the story of the benefits of the limes.

FIGURE 3: A sailed galleon.

Eating food

Digital ···· 4-5 ···

1 Imagine that you are a food scientist and you have just completed an investigation to show how saliva digests starch into sugar. Iodine was added to starch solution in a beaker, turning the iodine a blue-black colour. When amylase (the enzyme in saliva) was added and stirred, the blue-black colour disappeared.

Use the information above to design an easy-to-follow PowerPoint that will:

a Explain this change in colour to the reader.

b Explain to the reader what is happening at each stage in your own digestive system.

Test yourself ···· 5-6 ···

2 a Complete the labels on the diagram. Choose the words from the list below.

small intestine   large intestine   liver   stomach   oesophagus

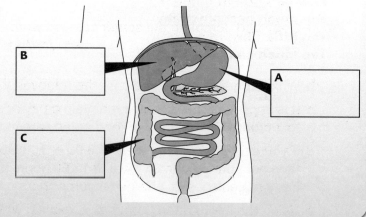

b Write the letter **D** where most of the digested food is absorbed into the blood stream.

c Digestion is the breaking down of large food molecules into smaller molecules. Explain why this is necessary.

d Name the chemicals produced in the body that speed up digestion.

Creative ···· 7-8 ···

3 Biological washing powders contain enzymes. It is the enzymes that digest the stains from dirty clothing, leaving them clean.

It is your task to design a role play and accompanying script in order to demonstrate to your classmates how the washing powder works to remove the stains.

Do I have enough energy?

4-5

Creative

1 Athletes require a diet made up from 57% carbohydrate, 30% fats and 13% protein so that they can train effectively.

Draw an illustrated pie chart of your favourite meal, using the nutritional information on the labels to calculate the energy value of your meal and the percentage of carbohydrates, fats and proteins.

(Hint: The nutritional information and energy values per portion given on the labels will help you in your task.)

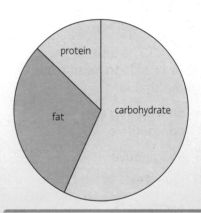

FIGURE 4: How does an athlete's diet differ from your own?

5-6

Test yourself

2 **a** Copy and complete the sentences and word equation for respiration, below.

Select your words from the following list (you may use a word more than once):

**water   carbon dioxide   carbon monoxide
oxygen   growth   warm   energy**

Food supplies your body with .... This energy is used in the body for movement, ... , repair and to keep us ....

.... + glucose ➡ .... + water + ... used for movement

b Explain why we need to eat more food in the winter.

c Explain why school children today may need less energy than they needed a generation ago.

d The government is concerned about the increasing level of obesity in young children in this country. What does this increase reveal about their diet?

7-8

Digital

3 We are very lucky in this country because children do not normally suffer from starvation.

a Research the consequences on the body of starvation in young children. Be sure to relate your research back to the energy requirements of young children.

b Present your findings as an illustrated article for a scientific journal.

KEEPING HEALTHY PROJECT

In groups, design a board game using the information that you have learned in the topic of Keeping Healthy.

Your brief is to design a game that is:

- challenging and competitive
- imaginative
- colourful
- exciting
- with aspects to suit a range of abilities
- able to be played by two or three teams of two players
- to take a period of approximately 15 minutes to play.

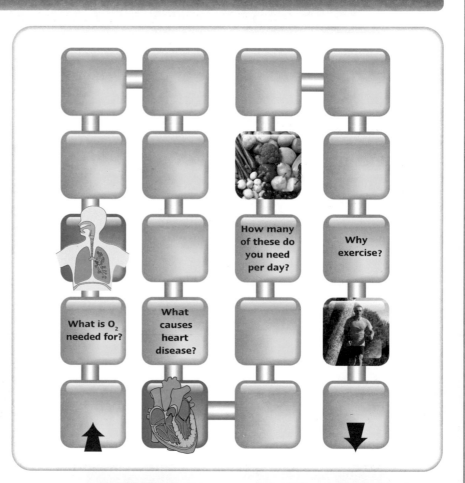

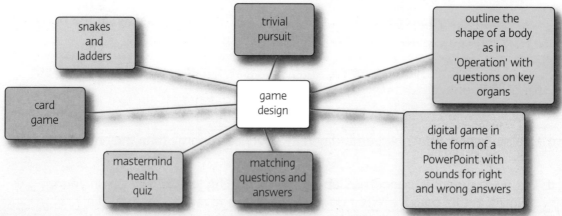

Planning

Brainstorm your ideas for **five** minutes and at the end of the time period choose **one** idea and stick to it.

Write out a selection of questions and answers – probably about 20 – ready for your game.

Allocate jobs that need to be completed in class or for homework to each member of your team.

Gather the materials needed to manufacture your game.

See pages 8–25 of your Pupil Book

A breath of fresh air

Creative

1 On Science Activity Day, your class teacher suggests that you compile a crossword (or word search with clues) using the key words about lungs, in order to test the knowledge and understanding of students at your neighbouring school.

Draw out your crossword (or word search) and write a list of clues. Be sure to have your answers prepared so that you can test another student's scientific knowledge!

Test yourself

2 a Copy the diagram below and complete the labels, choosing from the words below:

bronchus   right lung   trachea   alveoli   bronchiole

b What process describes how oxygen passes from the alveoli into the blood?

c Describe **one** feature of the alveoli that allows for the efficient exchange of gases between the air in the alveoli and the blood.

d What is the difference between breathing and respiration?

e The two types of specialised cells shown below are found in the lining of the lungs. Explain the role of the ciliated and mucus-producing cells in keeping the lungs clean.

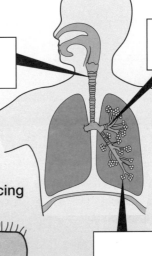

FIGURE 5: Mucus-producing cell (left) and ciliated cell (right), both found in the lungs.

Digital

3 Cancer Research UK reports that 450 children take up smoking in the UK every day. Internet research about children and smoking reveals complex and detailed webpages that are difficult to navigate.

Design your own webpage aimed at a teenage audience clearly pointing out the health risks linked to smoking. Use a combination of eye-catching design and high-impact scientific information.

A healthy heart

Creative

1 It is your task to produce a set of word and definition cards about the heart. (One card has the word and the other card has the definition.) Next lesson you can pair up with a classmate and use the cards to revise your knowledge of the heart.

Test yourself

2 a Fred is a lorry driver. He stops at roadside burger vans for his breakfast and lunch and chain-smokes on his long journeys. He develops pains in his chest and visits the doctor.

Match each substance or activity on the left to a statement on the right to show the effect of each on the body.

Fatty food	**reduces the availability of oxygen in the blood**
Lack of exercise	**causes damage to the coronary artery**
Carbon monoxide	**causes cancer**
Nicotine	**causes addiction to smoking**
Tar	**can lead to obesity**

b i Make a sketch of the diagram opposite. On your sketch draw in arrows to show the circulation of the blood through the heart.

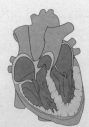

   ii Label the valves on the heart.

Digital

3 When listening to a patient's heart, a doctor detects a possible problem with one of the heart valves. Imagine that you are the doctor in this situation and that you wish to explain to the patient the role of the heart valves.

a Download a picture of the heart from the Internet.

b Prepare a PowerPoint slideshow for use on your surgery computer.

   i Using your downloaded image, show the pathway of the blood, the names of the blood vessels and the chambers of the heart in the correct sequence.

   ii Add to your slideshow an explanation of the role of the valves in the heart.

c Print off your slideshow and stick it into your exercise book.

Measuring your pulse

1 William Harvey was the first scientist to explain how blood is pumped around the body.

a Use the Internet to research the work of William Harvey.

(Hint: www.bbc.co.uk is a good starting point.)

b Armed with your research, imagine that you are William Harvey writing a letter to the Royal Society of Doctors about your amazing discovery. Explain the role of the heart and how pulse felt at the pressure points is due to the heart pumping the blood around the body.

FIGURE 6: William Harvey (holding an animal's heart) demonstrating his discovery to his fellow doctors.

2 **a** Draw a line graph showing your pulse rate as you ride your bicycle on the journey below. (Do not forget to place realistic values for your pulse rate on the graph.)

Stage 1	**Waiting at the traffic lights for 1 minute**
Stage 2	**Pedalling up a slight incline for 2 minutes**
Stage 3	**Racing your friend for a further 2 minutes**
Stage 4	**Freewheeling down a hill for 3 minutes**

b Design a key for each stage of the journey.

c Write a sentence explaining what is happening at each stage and why.

3 The graph opposite shows pulse rate during different activities.

a i Use the graph to find the pulse rate when resting.

ii Describe the relationship between the type of activity and the pulse rate.

iii If the person under investigation had been smoking for many years, how would you expect the pulse rate results to differ?

b When training in First Aid it is important that the ABC code is learnt to deal with a patient who is not breathing and whose heart has stopped beating. What does ABC stand for?

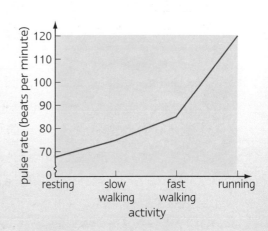

How do you know if you are fit?

Test yourself 4–5

1 a Sara decides to change her lifestyle and to begin a training programme. Which **three** things from the list below does she need for a healthy diet?

foods high in fats for energy **a balanced diet** **sugary drinks**
water **fibre** **chocolate**

b List the changes that happen to the body when you take part in a 100 metre sprint on sports day.

c What substances are transported around the body in the blood when exercising?

d When you are exercising, where in the body would most of your energy be used?

Creative 5–6

2 Design a bottle for a new sports drink that a runner could drink to hydrate and energise themselves during a marathon. Your design must give the nutritional content of the drink (including information on salts and glucose) and scientific information explaining the benefits of the drink to the athlete.

Digital 7–8

3 Produce a flow diagram using Word, clearly detailing the advice that you would give to a marathon runner about the nutrition and stages that should be involved in their training.

(Hint: www.eatwell.gov.uk will get you started on gathering information.)

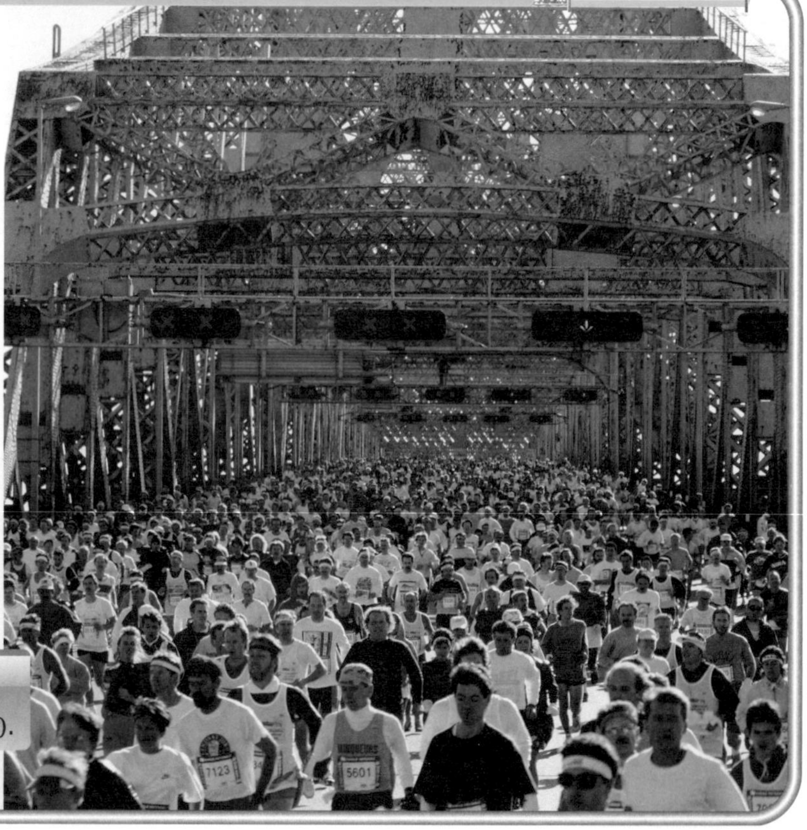

FIGURE 7: A runner must train very hard if they want to complete a marathon (26.2 miles).

See pages 24–25 of your Pupil Book

History of disease

4–5

Digital

1 Louis Pasteur was a great scientist and his scientific work is still important today in helping us to understand how microbes are responsible for disease. Research the work of Louis Pasteur, explaining why his experiments changed the way of thinking about the causes of disease.

(Hint: www.bbc.co.uk will provide you with a starting point for your research.)

FIGURE 1: A Polish postage stamp with an illustrated portrait of Louis Pasteur.

Test yourself

5–6

2 a Match the name of each scientist to their discovery.

Louis Pasteur	**Demonstrated that disease could be spread by contaminated water.**
John Snow	**Demonstrated that life was not created from rotting meat.**
Robert Koch	**Demonstrated the first vaccination.**
Edward Jenner	**Demonstrated that anthrax was spread by spores.**

b We continue to develop new theories about what causes certain diseases.

   i We now know that lung cancer is caused by cigarette smoke. How do you think doctors discovered the link between cigarette smoke and lung cancer?

   ii It has now been found that passive smoking can be responsible for increasing the chances of contracting lung cancer. How did scientists come to this conclusion?

Creative

7–8

3 Shoppers for milk can purchase pasteurised, sterilised or UHT milk.

   a Imagine that you are a microbiologist working in a milk dairy. Write up the experimental procedure for pasteurising milk. Be sure to list the equipment needed in the procedure and to include the temperatures involved at each stage.

   b Design an information leaflet to explain to customers the benefits of each type of milk.

FIGURE 2: Pasteurising milk.

The infection cycle

Creative

4-5

1 The poem opposite was written at the time of the Great Plague in London in 1665. Red blotches on the skin were symptoms of the disease; people thought that posies would protect them from catching the disease; finally, before death the victim sneezed a great deal!

Write a similar poem for a different disease, detailing how it is spread, the symptoms and how the body's immune system combats the disease.

> Ring-a-ring o'roses,
> A pocketful of posies,
> Atishoo, atishoo,
> We all fall down.

Digital

5-6

2 When children become ill it is useful to have a quick reference guide for the symptoms of diseases or allergies.

Produce a reference sheet designed for parents to download from the NHS website, showing the names of some common childhood diseases (such as measles, scarlet fever, mumps and whooping cough) and allergies (to substances such as nuts and pollen). Provide information on the symptoms and recommendations for combating the disease or allergy.

(Hint: www.nhsdirect.nhs.uk is a good starting point for your research.)

Test yourself

7-8

3 A bacterium is a single-celled structure, as shown below.

a Bacteria can live outside living cells. How do bacteria reproduce?

b How can a doctor treat a bacterial infection?

c When bacteria reproduce, they can change their genetic material. Why does this cause problems when treating a bacterial infection?

d A virus only reproduces inside a living cell. How does this cause problems for the doctor when treating a viral infection?

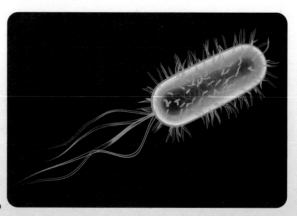

Preventing disease

1 Imagine that you are a scientist working in the health industry. You are asked to invent a new plaster that will reduce the possibility of infection. Draw your new product and explain how it will stop infection entering the wound and then help to reduce the chance of infection.

2 **a** A dressing or plaster will prevent a cut from becoming infected. Name **one** type of micro-organism which can infect the cut.

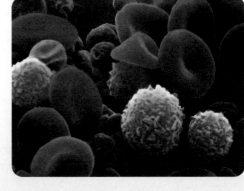

   b **i** Copy the photograph opposite as a simple diagram. Label the diagram showing the different parts of the blood.

      ii Which part of the blood shown in part **i** will play a part in fighting the infection?

      iii Which part of the blood will play a part in forming a scab?

   c The graph shows the number of bacteria in the body following a cut on broken glass.

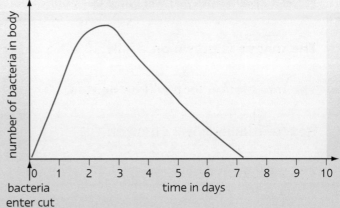

      i Use the graph to determine how long it took for the cut to become infected.

      ii Why did the wound heal after taking the antibiotics?

      iii Use the graph to suggest the number of days the antibiotics were taken for.

      iv Why is it important that the course of antibiotics is completed?

3 Design a new computer game called 'Body Attack'. Viruses and bacteria represent the invaders of the body. Your game must be exciting as well as educational, explaining how the body's defence system destroys the invaders.

You may wish to produce the game in PowerPoint, using images from the Internet.

Sexually transmitted diseases

Test yourself   4-5

1 a When identifying a sexually transmitted disease, a sample will be taken and grown on the surface of a jelly in a Petri dish.

   i What precautions will the doctor take when obtaining the sample?

   ii The sample will be taken with a cotton swab. Why is it important that the swab is sterile?

  b After a patient has been diagnosed with a sexually transmitted disease, it is very important that the patient's sexual partner visits a doctor immediately. Why do you think this is so?

  c Name the key sexually transmitted disease that cannot be cured.

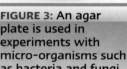

FIGURE 3: An agar plate is used in experiments with micro-organisms such as bacteria and fungi.

Creative   5-6

2 Imagine that you are a microbiologist with the task of testing a new cream to treat thrush, a skin fungal disease that can be sexually transmitted.

  a Explain how you will carry out your experiment by matching up the correct phrases.

The fungus is grown on a jelly		it prevents contamination.
The inoculation loop will be heated		it provides a fair test.
Repeat readings will be taken	**because**	it provides nutrients for fungal growth.
The Petri dish will be grown without the fungus		they show that readings are reliable.

  b Create a leaflet to be used as part of the advertising campaign for the cream that you have developed, detailing how you went about creating the product, how it will work and why it is the best product of its kind.

Digital   7-8

3 Use your powers of persuasion to explain why it is essential to practise safe sex. You must use this debate to focus upon the key scientific terms of the topic, while emphasising the dangers of the spread of HIV and other sexually transmitted diseases. Produce your work as a podcast.

See pages 38–39 of your Pupil Book

STUDYING DISEASE PROJECT

Throughout the topic Studying Disease, you will have learnt many new scientific facts and terms that will be useful to you outside of your Science lessons. Now is the perfect time to bring together all that you know (and perhaps learn something new!) so that you can deal with the topic of disease in class and at home!

1 Gather together information from the topic of Studying Disease.

2 Prepare a short presentation to give to your class. As part of your presentation you must:

- Write out your script in full.

- Create note cards for when you deliver your presentation.

- Produce a poster or PowerPoint to show while you give your presentation. (The display must have visual impact as well as giving **key scientific facts**.)

3 Prepare a short quiz (this should have a minimum of five to ten questions), along with separate answers, for your classmates to complete later.

4 Design a certificate as a prize for the winning student.

5 Now you must deliver the presentation that you have prepared to your class.

Handy hints:
- Your presentation should be clear and well organised.

- Use scientific terms.

- Try not to read from your script – use your note cards as prompts.

- Be energetic and enthusiastic!

6 Once you have completed your presentation, ask your audience the quiz questions.

7 Give the class the correct answers to the quiz and lead a brief class discussion on the ideas that came out of the quiz.

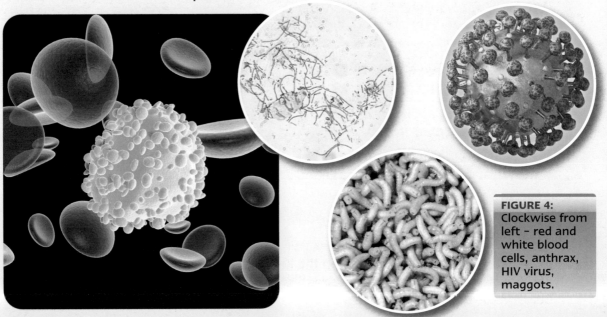

FIGURE 4: Clockwise from left – red and white blood cells, anthrax, HIV virus, maggots.

See pages 32–51 of your Pupil Book

Biological warfare

Creative

1 With the increased fear of biological warfare, your company decides to manufacture a biological suit that can be purchased by the public. Design your suit along with a sales leaflet pointing out to the public the features that will protect them against this pending threat!

Digital

5-6

2 Imagine that you are a scientist working in the field of germ warfare. Alarmingly, you discover that a terrorist group has developed a new germ warfare infection. You are tasked with writing a report describing its structure, symptoms, toxins, method of reproduction and how it could possibly be spread by the terrorist group. With this information, determine how the disease will be prevented from spreading to the population.

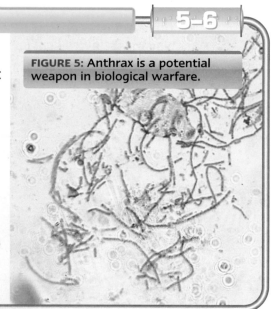

FIGURE 5: Anthrax is a potential weapon in biological warfare.

Display your findings as a podcast that can be immediately broadcast to governments around the world so that they can make preparations for the potential use of the germ warfare.

Test yourself

7-8

3 The graph opposite shows the increase in cases of a mysterious vomiting disease in a small number of government workers.

a Describe the trend in the number of infections from the disease.

b What action would you recommend to prevent the disease from spreading to other members of the public?

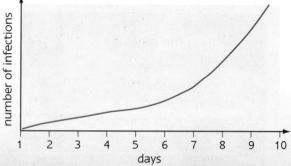

c Health scientists determine that the disease is very difficult to catch. Redraw the graph showing what would happen if the disease was easier to contract.

d Redraw the graph showing what would happen if a successful vaccine was developed for the disease.

e The government believes the disease may be a result of enemy government action – should they retaliate using biological warfare? Explain your answer in a maximum of 200 words.

Vaccination

1 Edward Jenner was a country doctor who developed a vaccination for smallpox. Create a 'History of Medicines' webpage for the school Science club explaining Edward Jenner's method of vaccination.

2 When Edward Jenner was investigating the vaccine for smallpox, he tested his theory by inoculating a small boy called James Phipps with the material from a cowpox blister. If James had died, Jenner would have risked being put on trial for murder!

Imagine that you are the judge in a court deciding if the experiment on young James should go ahead. Consider your verdict and write a letter explaining your decision to the newspapers of the day (they found Jenner's work very suspicious and openly criticised it!).

3 The graph opposite shows the number of people with measles.

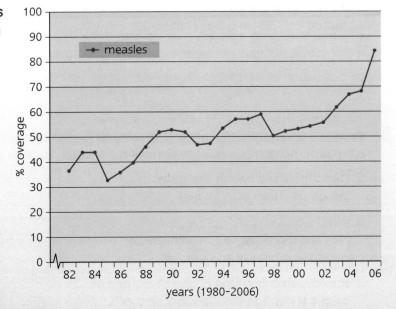

a What does 'immune' mean?

b Which part of the blood is responsible for fighting the measles infection?

c The government is currently running a campaign to encourage parents to make sure that their children are immunised against measles. Use the graph to explain why this new campaign is necessary.

d Redraw the shape of the graph if the government campaign is successful.

e If a small outbreak of measles occurs in an isolated area, what actions would you recommend to be taken?

What are vaccines?

1 a Link the terms on the right to the correct definition on the left.

White blood cells	Produced by white blood cells.
Antibiotics	Produce antibodies to attack the infection.
Antitoxins	Medicines used to treat bacterial infection.
Platelets	Weakened form of the disease introduced into the body.
Toxins	Responsible for forming a scab to seal a wound in the skin.
Vaccine	Poisons produced by microbes.

b When babies are born, they are sometimes immune to diseases such as measles for a short period of time without ever having been vaccinated against them. Why do you think this is so?

c When travelling abroad, why do you think it is necessary to seek information about the diseases that are most common in the countries that you are visiting?

Creative
5–6

2 Produce an imaginative and easy-to-read leaflet advising families about the vaccinations that are recommended for a range of holiday destinations around the world. Include information about the form that the vaccinations take and how they work.

Digital
7–8

3 Research shows that in the near future measles could become endemic in the UK. Create a webpage for the local doctor's surgery to address concerns that parents may have about vaccinations and to advise them of the importance of vaccinating their children against this disease.

(Hint: http://news.bbc.co.uk is good place to begin your research.)

FIGURE 6: Many diseases have been effectively wiped out through the use of vaccines.

See pages 46–47 of your Pupil Book

How to get rid of microbes

Creative 4-5

1 There has been an outbreak of infection at your local hospital. Imagine that you are the manager in charge of the hospital's cleaning team. Design a leaflet laying out a clear set of instructions to the cleaners that will explain:

- what cleaning products to use in particular areas
- where to clean
- what protective clothing to wear
- how to warn and protect the public.

Digital 5-6

2 Imagine that you are a TV producer with the brief of launching a new advertisement for a household cleaning product. You have a one minute airtime slot. It is important that your advert is scientific, includes information on health and safety, and is memorable and dynamic! Present your work as a podcast for distribution to TV companies.

Test yourself 7-8

3 A microbiologist is working on a treatment for a fungal infection. The fungus is grown on a jelly in a Petri dish.

The scientist places three small paper discs that have been treated onto the surface of the jelly. The diagram opposite shows the results of the experiment.

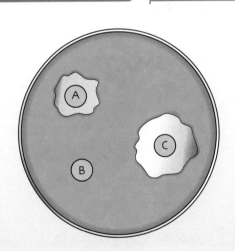

a Which disc has been soaked in distilled water?

b Why is there a clear area around the discs **A** and **C**?

c Which is the most effective treatment for the fungal infection?

d i What is the dependent variable in this experiment?

  ii What is the control variable in this experiment?

e Why would this experiment not work if the infection under investigation was caused by a virus?

f Microbiologists are constantly producing new antibiotics to fight the same type of bacterial infections. Explain why this is the case.

Are microbes useful?

1 Use the thermometer to identify the correct temperature:

a at which bread is left to rise before baking

b at which bacteria reproduce quickly

c at which bacteria are destroyed

d at which yoghurt should be stored

e of a refrigerator

f of a freezer.

Digital
5–6

2 Yeast is a microbe that has been used by man for thousands of years. Research and produce a timeline showing how the use of yeast has developed.

Creative
7–8

3 Imagine that you are a microbiologist working in a brewery. You are investigating the growth of a new strain of yeast. The graphs opposite show how the number of yeast cells increases when they are grown in a culture of glucose solution.

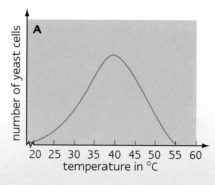

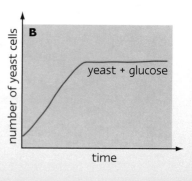

Use the following questions to write a report on your results for the magazine 'Food and Science Today'.

a Use graph **A** to describe how the number of yeast cells change with temperature.

b What temperature would you recommend for maximising the growth of yeast cells?

c Describe how the number of yeast cells change over the period of time in graph **B**.

d Why does the number of yeast cells in graph **B** not continue to increase?

See pages 50–51 of your Pupil Book

Dissolving rocks

4–5

Creative

1 Talk the formula!

Your Science teacher constantly refers to calcium carbonate as $CaCO_3$.

i Produce a script to explain to your class what the formula $CaCO_3$ actually represents.

ii Create a set of illustrations to go with your script and aid you in your explanation.

Hint: As a starting point you may wish to begin with CO_2 (carbon dioxide), explaining that it is made up from one atom of carbon and two atoms of oxygen. You could then progress to H_2O (water) and finally to $CaCO_3$, breaking down each formula into separate sections.

Test yourself

5–6

2 a In geography you are set the task of investigating the different types of rocks used for headstones in the cemetery. When looking at the inscriptions on some of the older gravestones, you notice that they are difficult to read. What rock are these gravestones more likely to be made from?

A Granite　　**B** Limestone　　**C** Marble

b You know that the cause of the erosion is likely to be acid rain. What is the main source of this acid rain?

c Copy and complete the word equation when sulphuric acid is added to calcium carbonate:

calcium carbonate + sulphuric acid ➔ .... + ... + water

Digital

7–8

3 Water is a universal solvent that dissolves many chemicals; however, in some areas of the country hard water can cause a potentially damaging build-up of calcium carbonate in washing machines.

You may have seen advertisements for water softening products on the television. It is your task to investigate the problems caused by hard water and also to find out about the level of water hardness and treatment in the home and in industry. (Hint: The website www.hardwater.org is a good starting point for your research.)

Present your work as a webpage for a water softening product, highlighting and illustrating the key facts about your product.

Sweet tooth

Creative

4-5

1 You are asked to bake an iced birthday cake for a party. When purchasing the ingredients you notice that there are three different types of sugar on the shelves: icing sugar, caster sugar and granulated unrefined cane sugar.

  a Research how to make the cake and decide which of the sugars you would buy, explaining your reasons.

  b Draw a poster for your school kitchen, to inform students on why certain sugars are used in baking.

Digital

5-6

2 Produce an easy-to-follow flow diagram in Word, illustrating the procedure used to produce rock candy crystals. It is important that you include:

  • equipment needed in manufacture

  • quantities of materials

  • time needed

  • possible risks to yourself or others.

  (Hint: A search for 'how to grow sugar crystals' on www.chemistry.about.com will assist you in gathering the written instructions.)

Test yourself

7-8

3 a The graph opposite shows the solubility of three chemicals at different temperatures.

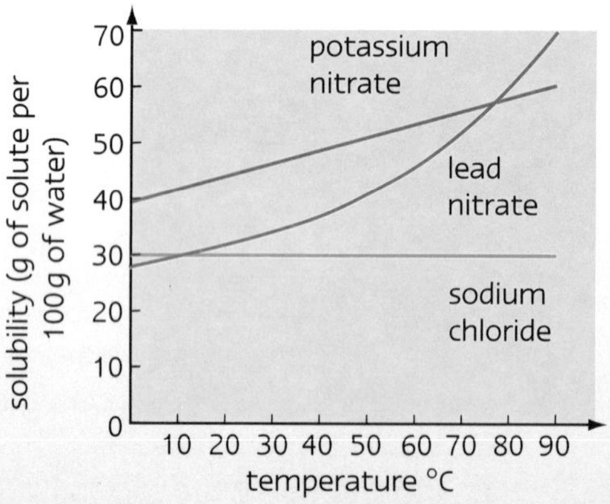

  i Explain how the solubility of each chemical changes with temperature.

  ii When completing the experiment, what piece of equipment would be necessary for maximum accuracy when adding the solutes?

  iii What is the independent variable in this experiment?

  iv What is the dependent variable in the experiment?

  b When dissolving sugar in a cup of cold water you find that, after adding two tablespoons of sugar, granules of sugar are still visible. What could you do to increase the solubility of the water?

  c You now repeat the investigation by adding salt to the cup. What difference would you see in your results? Explain your answer.

See pages 60–61 of your Pupil Book

Pure salt

1 a Copy the following sentence and fill in the gaps.

A solid that dissolves in a .... to form a solution is called a ....

b If you dissolved salt in water and wished to retrieve all of the salt, how would you do this?

c What safety precautions would you take?

2 You carry out the experiment below as part of an investigation. You must now convince your class that the salt has not disappeared! Find the most persuasive way to argue your case, using questions **a**, **b** and **c** to aid you.

a If you were instructed to taste the water in beaker 3, what would you find out?

b What would you notice about the readings on the electronic balances?

c What does this experiment tell us?

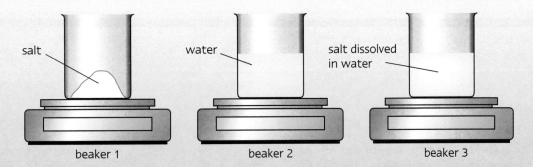

salt — beaker 1
water — beaker 2
salt dissolved in water — beaker 3

3 Produce an illustrated flow diagram in Word or PowerPoint clearly showing the stages and equipment used in the purification of rock salt.

You must:

- Add the key words in the process to your diagram: **soluble, evaporation, filtration, insoluble, boiling, crystallisation.**
- Add to your illustration 's' (solid), 'l' (liquid) or 'g' (gas) to show the states of matter at each stage.
- Draw in the arrangements of the particles at each stage.
- Include the health and safety precautions to be taken at different stages.

Super solvents

1 A student added some salt to water and stirred vigorously. He continued to add more salt until no more would dissolve. He then carried out the same exercise adding salt to alcohol, but found that the salt would not dissolve!

a Why did the salt not dissolve in the alcohol?

b Why did the student find that eventually no more salt would dissolve in water?

c How could the student alter the experiment so that more salt would dissolve in the water?

2 Your challenge is to produce a crossword in Excel, to be shared electronically with your class, for 10 to 15 of the key words encountered in the topic Separating Mixtures. Below are some of the key words you might like to include:

solvent	filtering	solid
solute	crystal	gas
solution	calcium carbonate	liquid
dissolve	stalactite or stalagmite	chromatography
soluble	condensation	separating
insoluble	boiling	salinity
universal solvent	steam	desalination

Remember to have your answers prepared so that you are able to reveal the correct answers to your classmates at the start of the next lesson.

3 Household cleaning products have warning signs on their packaging. Many cleaners contain solvents; for example, chlorine bleach to clean stains, and phosphates and phosphoric acid to clean toilets and remove limescale.

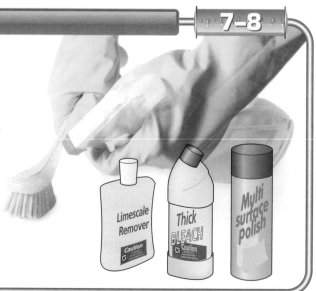

a Find out what the cleaners used in your home contain and if they are bio-friendly.

b Design your own cleaning product displaying the contents, how to use the product, health and safety advice and, if needed, a hazard warning label.

Distillation

Test yourself

1

a What process is taking place in the flask at **A**?

b Why is there cold water flowing through the water jacket?

c What temperature will the thermometer show?

d What is the name given to the apparatus?

e When distilling perfume, why would the temperature during the distillation process be a lot lower than when distilling salt water?

f When distilling perfume, why would it be dangerous to use a naked flame to heat the solution?

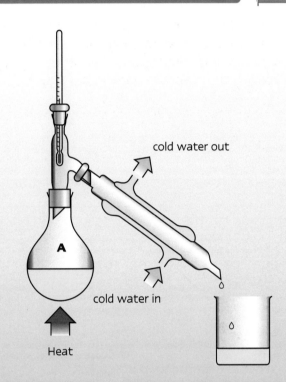

cold water out

A

cold water in

Heat

Creative

2 Create a role play for each of the different stages in the distillation of salt solution. Produce a script for each section. You must start with the dissolving of salt in water, then progress on to distillation, and finally pure water.

(Hint: The particle model at www.bbc.co.uk/schools/ks3bitesize may assist in your preparation.)

Digital

3 The scent and perfume industry has a huge customer base and is worth millions of pounds worldwide.

a Conduct Internet research into how perfume is manufactured using distillation. (Hint: www.madehow.com will assist in your research.)

b Design your own perfume or aftershave brand and create an electronic flyer to be used as part of a web campaign to explain the science behind fashion. On your flyer you must display the ingredients of your perfume or aftershave and explain how it is manufactured using scientific terms.

Better boiling

1

a Figure 1 shows apparatus that was used up until 1860 to distil liquids. Explain how this design was improved upon, in order to effectively turn vapours back into a liquid.

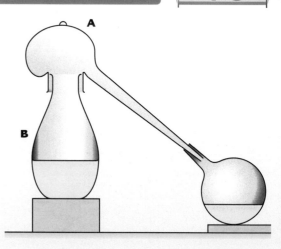

FIGURE 1: Early distillation apparatus.

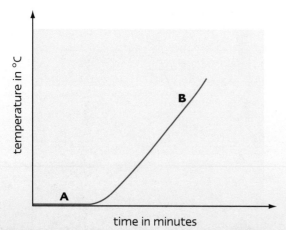

b The graph above shows how the temperature of water increases when ice is melted.

  i What is happening at stage **A**?

  ii What is happening at stage **B**?

  iii Copy and continue the graph when the water begins to boil.

  iv Show on the graph the temperature when the water boils.

2 Mountaineers encounter problems when cooking at high altitude because the reduction in atmospheric pressure lowers the boiling point of water. Using the Internet, research in greater depth the reason for the difficulties mountaineers encounter and explain how they produce hot meals.

3 Create your own wall display by completing **a** and **b** to help you to revise Better boiling and its links to the topic of Separating Mixtures.

  a In terms of molecular forces, explain why evaporation takes place faster at higher temperatures. Draw a diagram to illustrate your answer.

  b Sketch a graph showing the temperature changes during the distillation process.

SEPARATING MIXTURES PROJECT

North America and Australia are two industrial nations that are suffering drought conditions and hence water shortages. They require fresh water for drinking but, alarmingly, only one per cent of the Earth's water is fresh water. Desalination of seawater is a potential solution to the world's water shortage.

Design a home project kit that would provide your house with a fresh supply of drinking water.

It is important that your project includes the following aspects:

- a list of household equipment needed
- an illustration of your equipment, set up and ready for use
- a set of easy-to-follow instructions
- measurements that must be taken
- risks or potential dangers to the user and others
- safety precautions that must be taken
- storage instructions for the fresh water.

Prepare a short script in order to explain to your class how your fresh water device will work.

FIGURE 2: How can North America and Australia secure water supplies for the future?

Remember to include all of the scientific facts about changes of state and the way that the particles behave at each stage in the process.

See pages 58–75 of your Pupil Book

Drinking water

1

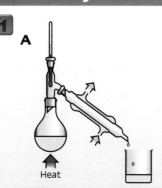

A

B

C

Heat

a What method of separation is shown in the three techniques above?

b Which piece of apparatus would be used to:

  i obtain salt crystals?

  ii produce water from ink?

  iii separate sand and water?

c i What is the process called that creates safe drinking water from seawater?

  ii Briefly describe this process.

2 The island of Malta in the Mediterranean is facing a major crisis in obtaining drinking water, especially in the height of the summer season when many holidaymakers arrive. The island obtains some of its water from desalination plants.

Imagine that you are the Senior Water Engineer in charge of future water supplies on Malta. Investigate the dilemma that Malta is facing in the light of climate change. Write a report clearly expressing your opinions based upon scientific facts. Post your report as a wiki.

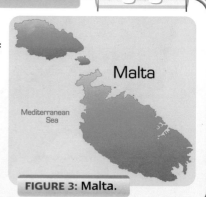

FIGURE 3: Malta.

3 There is a wide variety of drinking waters that can be purchased: mineral, spring, sparkling, well and fluoridated water. However, there are ethical issues regarding the purchase of such bottled water in the light of climate change, the energy crisis and the use of additional resources when tap water is readily available and considerably cheaper. Write an essay expressing your own opinions about which type of drinking water is best, both practically and ethically.

See pages 72–73 of your Pupil Book

Chromatography

Creative

1. **a** The picture card opposite contains a hidden word.

   i Identify the pictures (they show the name of a process or object).

   ii The number in the box refers to the key letter in the word. Use the key letters to find the hidden word.

   b Now make your own picture card on the science used in Separating Mixtures.

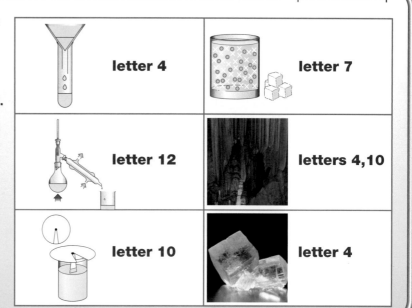

letter 4	letter 7
letter 12	letters 4,10
letter 10	letter 4

Test yourself

2. A forensic scientist finds the following chromatography results when investigating the ink from a pen found at the scene of a crime. He compares the ink with a set of three pens that the police found at the suspect's home.

   a Which coloured ink only contains **one** dye?

   b Which solvent would be used in the experiment: alcohol, water or acetone?

   c What is the colour of the ink that matches the pen found at the suspect's home?

   d Why is a pencil line used to locate the original ink spots at the beginning of the procedure rather than an ink pen?

Inks found at the crime scene

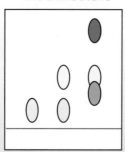

blue   green   brown

Inks found at the suspect's home

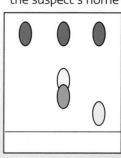

1   2   3
pens

Digital

3. Design an animated PowerPoint on chromatography displaying how different inks separate. Explain the reasons why the inks separate at different rates.

Chemical alphabet

4-5

Digital

1 You may not think it, but your kitchen is a mini-chemical laboratory and every time you cook and bake you are using chemicals and performing chemistry!

a Using the Internet to help you, research the chemistry that happens in your kitchen and then use Excel to copy and complete the table below.

Use	Chemical	Points of interest
Gas produced by yeast in baking		
Added to cake mixtures to make cakes rise		Alfred Bird invented custard and later developed this substance!
Used to sweeten food		
A metal used to wrap food to keep it fresh		
Used to kill microbes		
Added to orange juice		

b Now conduct further Internet research to find some of your own examples.

Test yourself

5-6

2 a Copy the table below and match the symbols to the correct element.

Mg   C   Cl   Cu   Au   Fe   Ag   Ca   O

Element	Symbol	Element	Symbol	Element	Symbol
Carbon		Gold		Silver	
Magnesium		Iron		Calcium	
Copper		Chlorine		Oxygen	

b Now add some examples of your own.

c $C_6H_{12}O_6$ is the chemical formula for glucose. State the number of atoms of each type in glucose and the total number of atoms in a molecule of glucose.

Creative

7-8

3 Research a chemical element – perhaps a metal such as copper, which is thought to have first been used by man in 9000 BC! Then, write a scientifically factual story about how that element has been developed and why it is important to mankind today. Make your story adventurous, dynamic and full of exciting science, developing the importance of the element!

See pages 82–83 of your Pupil Book

Getting sorted

1   **a** Draw a line from each element to the reason for using that element.

Copper in an electrical wire	Magnetic
Aluminium in a saucepan	Does not react with oxygen
Gold in jewellery	Good conductor of heat
Iron in a compass needle	Good conductor of electricity

b The diagram opposite shows the outline of the Periodic Table of Elements.

Match the following descriptions to region **A**, **B**, **C** or **D** of the Periodic Table:

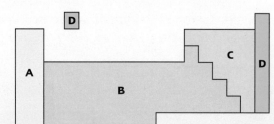

Hydrogen	
Non-metals	Very reactive metals
Metals	Inert gases

c Li is a reactive chemical. The element sodium (Na) is in the same column of the Periodic Table as Li. What properties is sodium likely to have?

2 Make a paper model of the regions of the Periodic Table and colour in the sections as in your Pupil Book on page 85. Make a set of 10 to 15 elements on squares of paper. Test a classmate to see if they can locate them correctly on your model. Use an assortment of the familiar and unfamiliar elements to make it a challenge!

3 Using www.periodic-table.org.uk and online scientific photo libraries to help you, make a set of illustrated fact cards on the elements found in the Periodic Table to create a matching game.

Example: Element: Oxygen   Clue: Makes up 21% of the atmosphere.

Select familiar and unfamiliar elements to stretch your knowledge, but remember that if you make your information too complicated you will spoil the game.

ATOMS, ELEMENTS AND COMPOUNDS PROJECT

The British Olympic cycling team brought back 14 medals from the 2008 Olympics in China. Their success was mainly due to intensive training and skill. However, the materials used in the building of their racing bicycles also had a part to play in their wins.

Materials technology is vital to the development of a product.

It is your project to research:
- the elements found in materials that are used in the manufacture of technology
- the properties that these elements give to the materials.

Consider a range of items that we use in our everyday lives and that are part of exciting technologies.

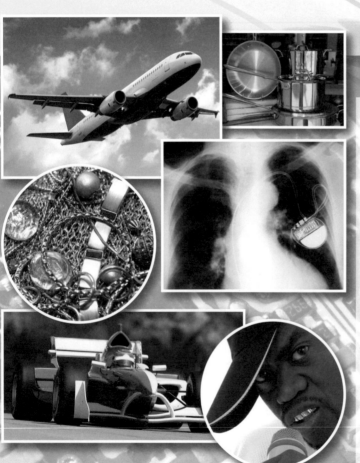

Following your research you must design a product launch for one of the products that you have researched.

The launch should include:
- a speech persuading buyers to purchase your product, based on scientific fact
- a presentation giving a breakdown of the materials in your product
- a demonstration of how materials technology helps your product
- an exciting, scientifically informative product leaflet.

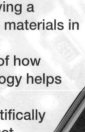

Start your search at www.epic-cycles.co.uk to find out about the elements used in the manufacture of the modern-day racing cycle.

See pages 82–95 of your Pupil Book

All mixed up

1 Copy and complete the table to create a poster for display in your Science laboratory that illustrates examples of mixtures and how they can be separated.

Mixture	Illustration	Separation technique
Iron and sulphur		
Sand and water		
Iron and lead		Use a magnet to attract and separate the iron from the lead

2 **a** Identify the following as elements, mixtures or compounds:

 Sea water   **Chlorine**   **Rust**   **Sodium chloride**
 Glucose   **Copper**   **Nitrogen**   **Carbon dioxide**

 b i Give **two** important properties of mixtures.

  ii Suggest how you would recognise that iron sulphide is not a mixture.

  iii Air is a mixture of different gases. What method is used to separate the gases in air?

3 Air is made from only a couple of different elements. Amazingly, the human body is also made from a very small number of elements that are mixed and joined together to make a human being. Research the chemicals found in the human body and draw a pictogram of the composition of chemicals in the body. Share your pictogram on a class wiki.

(Hint: Search online at www.chemistry.about.com to help you in your research.)

What are compounds?

4-5

Creative

1 When heated in a flame, certain chemicals burn spectacularly and with different colours. Fireworks are precisely filled with a chemical concoction to produce a particular effect (apart from the tremendous explosion!). The different colours are produced by an array of chemicals:

Silver	Magnesium or aluminium
Yellow	Sodium chloride
Orange	Calcium chloride
Red	Lithium carbonate
Blue	Copper chloride

Use the information above to draw a design for a firework showing the effects that you wish to create! Use the correct chemical symbols and explain the coloured effects of your creation!

Digital

5-6

2 Research and make a model of a chemical compound. You must also produce a wiki about your chemical compound, including information about how the compound is formed, its chemical symbol, properties and uses.

Image sites on the Internet will help in your research. Try to be adventurous in your choice rather than making the task too simple!

Test yourself

7-8

3

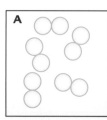
A

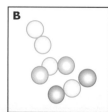
B

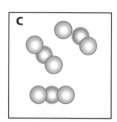
C

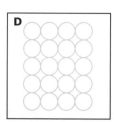
D

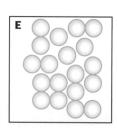
E

a Which of the boxes above shows:

   i oxygen   ii a mixture   iii copper   iv a liquid   v a compound?

b Copy and complete the sentences below.

   When two or more .... join together, a .... is formed. Iron
   .... is a .... formed from iron and oxygen, and iron sulphide is
   a compound formed from iron and ....

See pages 90–91 of your Pupil Book

Understanding equations

1 A strip of magnesium ribbon is placed into a ceramic crucible and heated with a strong Bunsen flame.

  a During the experiment the lid of the crucible is lifted slightly to allow the magnesium to react with a gas in the air. What is the name of this gas?

  b Write the word equation for this reaction.

  c i A white ash is left once the magnesium has completely burned. Would this weigh more or less than the weight of the magnesium ribbon at the start of the experiment?

    ii Explain your answer to part **i**.

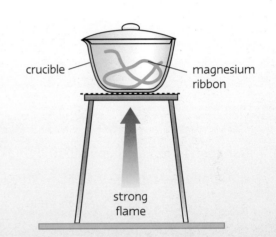

crucible — magnesium ribbon

strong flame

2 Chemistry is all around us! The climate is changing due to global warming; acid rain falls from our skies; our own bodies are chemical factories digesting our food and producing energy for movement and warmth; and we experience chemistry even when we barbecue or light a firework.

It is your task to research chemical equations that are important to society and humans. Research your examples on the Internet and produce your work as a Word presentation that can be shared electronically with your class.

Here are some examples that you may wish to include:

how acid rain is formed   **extraction of iron from iron ore**

photosynthesis   **magnesium in a firework**

burning natural gas   **respiration**

rusting

3 Make up a set of **six** chemical equation cards with matching right- and left-hand sides of the equation. Make **three** word equation sets and then progress onto making chemical symbol sets. You can use them to test a classmate's knowledge next lesson!

Combining elements

1 Produce an alphabet game for the words that you have used in this topic. Prepare the meaning for each word and pair up with a classmate to see how many of the 26 words you both know.

    Example: **A – atom – atoms are found in elements**

2 The following are all compounds:

CO_2 NaCl Na_2SO_4 CO $C_6H_{12}O_6$ Na_2CO_3 NO_2 CH_4 H_2O_2

For each compound you must:

a Identify the number and name of each atom in the compound.

b Identify the ratio of atoms in the compound.

c Use a scientific photo library (such as www.sciencephotolibrary.com) to find an image of the structure of the compound.

Produce your work as a table in Word, so that it can be added to and shared with your class throughout the topic.

3 Sulphur dioxide is a chemical compound used as a preservative and in wine-making to kill microbes. It is produced by volcanoes and can be manufactured in industry by burning sulphur.

a Write out the word equation for the production of sulphur dioxide.

b The diagrams opposite show the particle models of substances that take part in the reaction that produces sulphur dioxide.

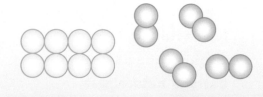

A   B

    i What does substance **A** represent in the reaction?

    ii What does substance **B** represent in the reaction?

c In the reaction, the compound sulphur dioxide is formed. Draw the compound of sulphur dioxide.

d Hydrogen oxide is a vital compound needed by all animals and plants on the planet! Write out the symbol equation for the formation of hydrogen oxide.

e What is the common name for hydrogen oxide?

See pages 94–95 of your Pupil Book

Magnetic materials

1
  a How would you test the piece of metal to determine whether it is a magnet or not?

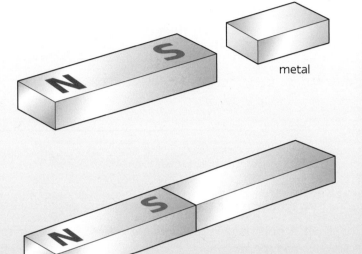

metal

  b Two magnets are placed together as shown in the diagram below.

    i Label the poles on the second magnet.

    ii A piece of aluminium is now placed next to the magnet. It is not attracted to the magnet. Explain why.

    iii Name another material that is magnetic.

2 Your school may use a magnetic whiteboard. Design a set of magnetic shapes – similar to those used as fridge magnets – that could be used in class to teach the topic of Magnetism.

Note: If your school does not have a magnetic whiteboard, you could use tack when you come to display your work.

3 During the Second World War many merchant and navy vessels were destroyed at sea by magnetic mines.

  a Research online how the magnetic mines worked to devastating effect and the method used to demagnetise the ships.

  b Present your findings as an animated PowerPoint slideshow.

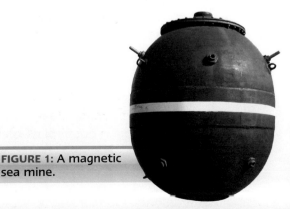

FIGURE 1: A magnetic sea mine.

Magnetic fields

1 Iron filings are sprinkled on a piece of paper placed over a magnet.

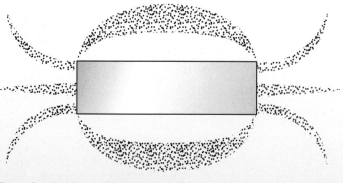 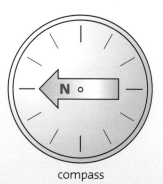

compass

a What do the iron filings show?

b A compass is placed near one of the poles as shown above. Label the poles on the magnet.

c Use this information to show which direction the force lines will point on the iron filings.

2 Draw a poster for display in your Science laboratory showing the magnetic fields and the direction of the magnetic field lines between:

a Like poles.

b Unlike poles.

c A single bar magnet.

3 Research the use of MRI (Magnetic Resonance Imaging) in medicine. Use your research to explain how MRI is used and to describe the advantages of MRI over X-rays.

Present your work as an information leaflet for hospital patients, designed to be downloaded from a hospital website.

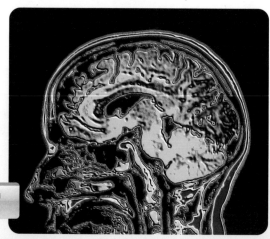

FIGURE 2: An MRI scan of the human brain.

Earth's magnetic field

1 The Earth behaves as if it had a giant bar magnet at its centre.

   a Label the poles on this magnet.

   b Draw in the direction of the magnetic field.

   c Draw in the location of the geographic North pole.

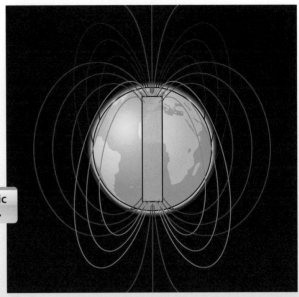

FIGURE 3: The magnetic field around the Earth.

2 Scientists believe that the Earth has at its centre a dense, fluid outer core that surrounds a solid inner core, both of which have iron-rich materials in them. The inner core is under such high pressure that it remains solid. The outer core is so hot that it is molten (liquid). When heated, the material in the molten outer core expands, becomes less dense and rises to the surface. Cooling at the surface causes the material to contract, become dense and sink once again, creating convection currents. The Geodynamo theory suggests that it is the movement of molten iron in the outer core (caused by the Earth's rotation), combined with the convection currents (caused by the heat of the inner core), that create a magnetic field in the molten iron.

You must now interpret this information to draw a labelled diagram of the Earth that will explain the theory behind the Earth's magnetic field. Start with a circle for the Earth and add the features described.

3 Imagine that you run a website for the school astronomy club. Design a homepage for your website, enhancing it with photographs to show different aspects of magnetism in the Solar System. Explain your chosen photographs with well-researched captions.

Hint: The 'Science and space' section of the National Geographic website (www.nationalgeographic.com) is a good starting point for your research.

Explaining magnetism

1 Little groups of atoms in magnetic material behave as tiny magnets. These groups are called 'magnetic domains'.

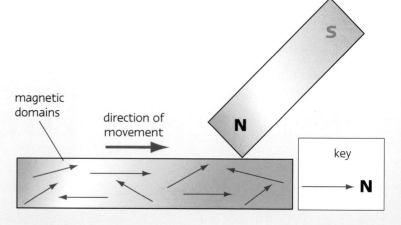

a A magnet is stroked across the surface of a magnetic material. Redraw the magnetic domains.

b Where is the magnetic field strongest?

c Another method of creating a magnet is to stroke the magnetic material from the centre, outwards. Label the ends of the magnets at X and Y.

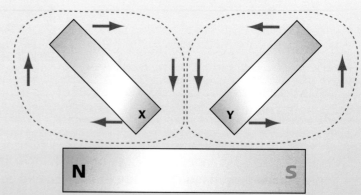

2 Create a role play as a starter activity for your next lesson to explain:

Either the domain theory of magnetism

Or the ways in which materials can be magnetised.

Write down your script and be prepared to demonstrate your role play to the rest of the class.

3 A new school laboratory technician has noticed that after a period of time the school magnets become weaker and that soft iron rods become magnetic when stored next to the magnets.

Use the Internet to research how the laboratory technician should store the magnets and why the soft iron rods become magnetic. Then, to be helpful to the new technician, prepare an e-mail attachment explaining your research in terms of **magnetic domains** and suggesting how they can demagnetise the soft iron rods by using a solenoid.

Electromagnetism

Creative

1 Scrap metal merchants and metal recycling companies use electromagnets attached to a crane to pick up scrap metal. Create a poster for a display in your Science laboratory illustrating applications of science in industry. Your poster should explain how electromagnetism can be used to:

- pick up the scrap
- adjust the strength of the magnetism
- release the load of iron into a crusher.

Hint: You may find it helpful to draw a symbol diagram of the electrical circuit.

Test yourself

2 In an experiment, insulated wire is wound around a nail made from steel to make an electromagnet. The magnet is used to pick up paperclips.

a Give **two** ways to adjust the strength of the magnetism.

b In the experiment, how would you judge the strength of the magnetism?

c When the switch is opened and the electromagnet is switched off, it is noticed that not all of the paperclips drop off. Explain why.

d What material could be used to replace the steel nail so that all of the paperclips are released when the electricity is switched off?

e If the nail was replaced with a copper bar, what would you notice?

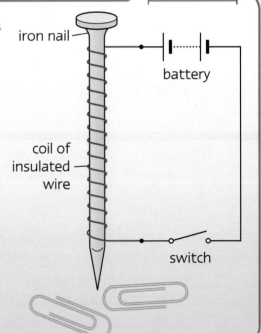

iron nail

battery

coil of insulated wire

switch

Digital

3 In industry when drilling, cutting and shaping metal, a risk assessment will be carried out to protect workers from flecks of iron and steel that may enter the eye. However, despite the precautions taken, accidents happen and metals can enter the eye!

Research how iron filings can be removed from the eye using electromagnetism. Use a PowerPoint to explain the advantages of using an electromagnet and why a permanent magnet cannot be used.

Using electromagnets

1 Your teacher asks you to produce a word search for use as a starter activity for next lesson. Using Word or Excel, you should produce a word search using the key words from the topic of Electromagnetism. You must also produce a highlighted version showing the answers so that you can mark their completed word searches. Share your word search with your class electronically.

2 Design an electromagnetic gadget to be used in the home, in industry or by a very lazy person! You must show the inside workings of the device and explain thoroughly how it works. Present your work as a leaflet advertising your invention.

Here are just a few ideas to get you started: a cat flap, a levitating novelty metal pen holder, a door lock, a desk drawer lock with hidden switch release, a buzzer, a burglar alarm, a relay to control an electric motor in a lift.

3 In an investigation, iron filings are used to determine the strength of an electromagnet. The number of coils of wire around the soft iron bar is adjusted.

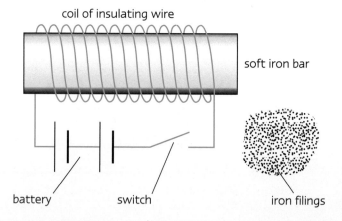

coil of insulating wire
soft iron bar
battery   switch   iron filings

  a i What is the independent variable in the experiment?

    ii What is the dependent variable in the experiment?

    iii Name **one** control variable in the experiment.

b Why are electromagnets more useful in industry than permanent magnets?

c When cutting the grass with an electric lawn mower it is essential to use a circuit breaker (Figure 4). If the gardener accidentally cuts the cable, a large current will flow through the live wire. How will the circuit breaker cut off the electricity supply?

d Steel is a magnetic material but is not used in the core of electromagnets. Explain why this is so.

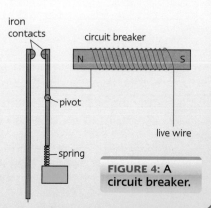

iron contacts
circuit breaker
N   S
pivot
live wire
spring

FIGURE 4: A circuit breaker.

See pages 112–113 of your Pupil Book

Motors and generators

1 Michael Faraday discovered how to generate electricity using magnetism.

Imagine that you are Michael Faraday. Write a letter to the Royal Institute of Physicists to explain your discovery and how you think it will change the world. Be sure to make your letter dynamic and full of excitement for the future!

Present your work as an e-mail to a friend who missed the topic on Motors and generators.

2 A bicycle dynamo can be used on a bicycle to power the front and rear lights. A friction wheel touches the front tyre, rotating a magnet inside a coil.

The graph opposite shows the brightness of the lamps on a journey. Explain what is happening at each stage of the journey.

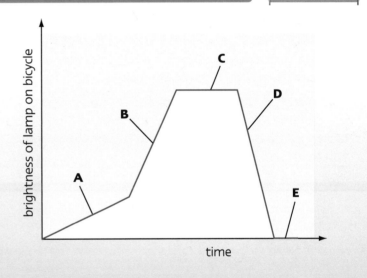

3 Bicycle dynamos can be very dangerous. Write an article for the school newspaper that:

a Explains the dangers of the dynamo.

b Suggests a technical solution to these potential dangers.

c Points out their advantages.

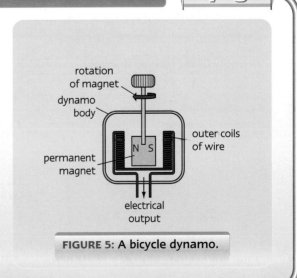

FIGURE 5: A bicycle dynamo.

MAGNETISM PROJECT

The government is looking for more sources of renewable energy to make sure that we will always have enough energy to meet our needs in the future. One renewable energy source that the government is keen to develop is **wind power**. However, the development of wind farms to generate electricity is not welcomed by everyone!

Read the newspaper articles on wind farms (in the Appendix, pages 84 and 85).

Brainstorm:

- the key words in the articles

- the key point in each paragraph

- what the articles are telling you.

In the form of a newspaper story, write your own response to the articles. Be sure to consider which article you believe and to explain whether you are for or against the building of more wind farms.

You must now find a group of four or five other students with the same view as yourself and prepare a short presentation arguing your point of view using the information that you have gathered.

You must include:

- scientific evidence to support your argument

- facts and figures to support your argument.

How to gain a high grade:

- Write the newspaper story in your own words.

- Use scientific words and terms.

- Include facts and figures.

- Write in well-structured, punctuated sentences, taking great care with your spelling.

- Take care with your presentation.

Power stations

1. Use the key words below to label the diagram of the power station.

   turbine   boiler

   furnace   fuel supply

   generator   steam

   condensor

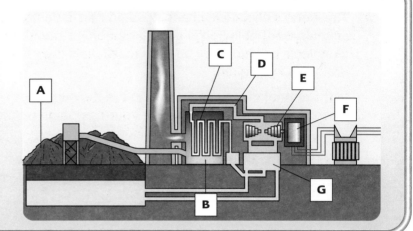

2. Demonstrate your sequencing skills in describing a physical process by explaining where electricity comes from when produced from fossil fuels. Present your information in an easy-to-learn PowerPoint.

   Use the key words below to help you in your description.

   fossil fuels turbine coal gas oil generator magnet heat energy steam magnet rotates coil furnace water condensor National Grid

3. Fossil Power is an energy company that wishes to build a new coal-fired power station in Northern Britain.

   Imagine that you are the head of your neighbourhood group and do not wish to have the power station built in your area.

   a Research the proposed power station and its location, and prepare a speech against the power station to deliver at your next District Council meeting.

   b To accompany your speech, create a newsletter to be sent to those people in the area that could not attend the meeting.

FIGURE 6: Imagine a coal-fired power station such as this one near your home.

Burning problems

1 The world's climate is changing: acid rain is destroying the habitats of plants and animals, soot pollution is affecting people's breathing in some major cities, and other chemicals produced by burning fossil fuels have resulted in increased asthma problems in children.

In the school mock elections, you are the campaign organiser for the 'Green Friendly Earth' party. Design a poster for your campaign pointing out the effects that burning fossil fuels is having upon the planet.

Marks will be awarded for scientific content and high-impact presentation.

2 When we burn fossil fuels we produce large amounts of pollution.

a Which fossil fuels do we burn to generate electricity?

b Coal produces large amounts of sulphur dioxide. Copy and complete the word equation below.

.... + ... ➞ sulphur dioxide

c What problem does the production of sulphur dioxide lead to?

d Burning fossil fuels also produces carbon dioxide. Copy and complete the word equation below.

fossil fuel + ... ➞ carbon dioxide + ... + energy

e What problem is created by the production of this carbon dioxide?

3 Acid rain blown across the North Sea is having an effect upon the lakes and fjords in Norway and Sweden.

a Write a script for a brief but high-impact video on the effects of acid rain upon the planet.

b Draw out the film sequence for your video as a PowerPoint slideshow.

You may wish to share your video as a podcast.

See pages 120–121 of your Pupil Book

Renewable energy resources

4–5

Test yourself

1 The list below shows a selection of energy sources:

A Coal   **B** Hydroelectric   **C** Gas   **D** Wind power   **E** Geothermal   **F** Bio-fuel   **G** Tidal

a Which of the energy sources are non-renewable?

b Which of the energy sources involve kinetic energy?

c What is the name of the renewable energy source that uses heat in rocks?

d What are the energy changes that occur in hydroelectric power stations?

e Which renewable energy source will both remove carbon dioxide and then release carbon dioxide into the atmosphere?

Creative

5–6

2 Renewable energy sources greatly reduce the damage caused to our planet by burning fossil fuels.

Imagine that you are an engineer specialising in renewable energy. You are called in to develop the future renewable energy resources for a small island population. Copy the diagram of the island and explain where you would locate the different renewable sources listed below and why, giving the advantages and disadvantages of each.

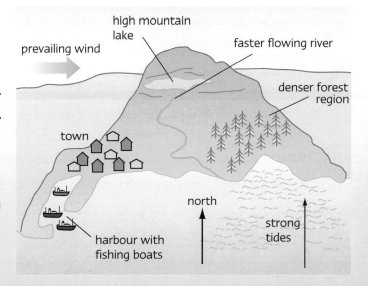

prevailing wind
high mountain lake
faster flowing river
denser forest region
town
north
strong tides
harbour with fishing boats

Wind   Solar   Hydroelectric   Bio-fuel   Tidal barrage   Wave generator

Digital

7–8

3 Britain is an island that receives strong winds blowing in from across the Atlantic Ocean, causing large waves. Imagine that the government is keen to take advantage of this renewable energy resource and to develop wave power in this country.

Research the potential locations for wave power stations in Britain and explore the advantages and disadvantages of generating electricity from waves. Use your findings as part of a 'Save the Planet' campaign, designed to be posted on your school website.

What about nuclear power?

Digital 4–5

1 The energy debate has increased urgency if Britain is to secure its future electricity supplies. Have your say by using the Electricity Calculator on the BBC website.

You can access the Electricity Calculator by the quick link http://newsvote.bbc.co.uk/1/shared/spl/hi/uk/06/electricity_calc/accessible/default.stm. Alternatively you can access it by:

- Going to the BBC news page.
- Clicking on 'Special Reports' on the left-hand tool bar.
- Selecting 'Climate change' from the 'Science/Nature/Technology' drop-down menu at the bottom of the page and clicking 'Go'.
- Find the section 'You and climate change' at the bottom of the page and click to 'Decide where the UK's energy comes from'.

By using the drop-down menu, you can vote on how you would like future electricity to be generated. Write a short report on how you voted, along with your scientific reasons.

Test yourself 5–6

2 **a** Nuclear power stations do not produce polluting gases. However, they do cause other problems. What are these problems?

b In a nuclear power station what replaces the furnace?

c Why is global warming not a problem when electricity is produced by a nuclear power station?

d Nuclear power stations have high de-commissioning costs. What is de-commissioning?

Creative 7–8

3 Energy experts believe that within ten years Britain will be suffering electricity blackouts just like those being experienced in large cities in America today. In the light of this alarming fact, the government is keen to promote the building of nuclear power stations to provide enough electricity to meet increases in demand. However, there is opposition to this plan by Greenpeace and Friends of the Earth.

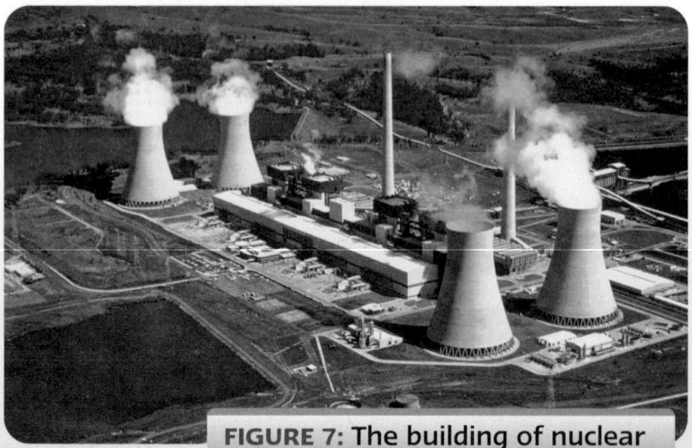

FIGURE 7: The building of nuclear power stations is controversial.

Write an essay considering these opposing views and making clear your own opinions on this important issue.

See pages 124–125 of your Pupil Book

What is sound?

1

a Light and sound are two types of energy that travel as waves. Light energy can travel through space and through a vacuum. Why can sound not travel through space?

b When a guitar is played the strings are plucked.

  i How can a player make the guitar sound louder?

  ii The player alters the length of the strings. What effect does this have on the sound?

  iii The strings of the instrument are of different thicknesses. What is the difference in the sound between plucking a thick string and a thin string?

  iv When tuning the guitar one of the strings is tightened. What effect will this have on the sound?

FIGURE 1: Guitars produce music when the strings vibrate.

Creative 5-6

2 By placing a piece of paper along the prongs of a hair comb, a simple but effective musical instrument can be created. Make a drawing of this simple instrument and explain how it can be used to produce sound of different musical notes with varying loudness.

Digital 7-8

3 Many musical instruments use a sound box to improve the quality of the sound.

  a Research the role of the sound box on the Internet.

  b Download an image of your favourite stringed musical instrument.

  c Using your research and the facts that you have learnt on sound, explain how the instrument works. Produce your work as a revision document that can be stuck in your exercise book.

Describing sounds

Digital 4-5

1 **Note:** You must ask your teacher for permission to use a mobile phone for this homework.

Use a mobile phone to make recordings of sounds of different pitches and loudness. Prepare explanations of the features (including the frequency and wavelength) of the different sounds for next lesson.

Creative 5-6

2 There are lots of new terms used in the topic of Sound.

You decide to help yourself and your classmates learn these terms by producing a quick revision quiz. Make sure that you have the correct answers prepared for when you try out your quiz next lesson!

Test yourself 7-8

3 A loudspeaker and signal generator are connected to an oscilloscope. The different wave patterns are shown below.

A
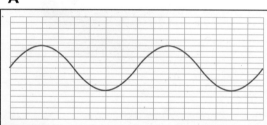

B
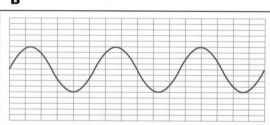

C
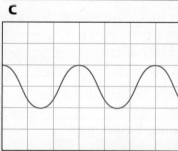

D
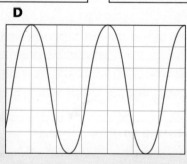

E
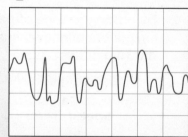

a Identify the loud sound. A

b Identify the high frequency sound. D

c How does trace **A** on the oscilloscope differ from trace **B**? B is picking up more sound

d Copy trace **D** and draw in the amplitude of the wave.

e The volume of the sound is gradually turned down from maximum volume until the sound is turned off. Draw the shape of the wave pattern on the oscilloscope.

f Trace **E** shows the pattern of the speaking voice. Why is the pattern so irregular?

Speed of sound

1 During a firework display, two types of energy are produced that travel by waves.

a What are the **two** types of energy? *sound, light*

b Why do you see the firework before you hear the explosion? *because the light travels quicker then the sound*

c If you walk away from the firework display the explosions are quieter. Explain why. *sound*

d Do sound waves travel quicker in solids or in liquids? *liquid*

e The Sun is a huge star producing enormous explosions and yet we cannot hear it. What does this tell you about the light from the Sun? *the light travels further then the sound*

2 Supersonic aeroplanes travel at speeds greater than Mach 1.

a Use the Internet to find out what the term 'Mach 1' means.

b i Describe what happens to the speed of sound at higher altitudes.

ii Present your answer as a PowerPoint, using an image of a globe to show the speed of sound at different altitudes.

iii Now use the particle theory to add an explanation of your research to your PowerPoint.

3 **a** Your teacher sets you the task of copying and completing the table below to calculate the speed of sound.

i Use the formula triangle to calculate the missing values. Then fill in the final column to show if the sound is travelling in a solid, liquid or gas.

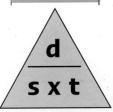

ii Draw a graph illustrating the speed of sound in solids, liquids and gases.

Speed (m/s)	Distance (m)	Time (s)	Solid, liquid, gas
400	1650	5.0	
320	1000	10:24	
1500	3000	2.0	
4300	0.01	43	
200	1000	0.2	

b Imagine that you are on a deep-sea fishing trawler. Produce an illustration for the boat's wheel house to show the captain at what depth to lower his nets to catch fish. You are told that the ultrasonic pulse from the ship's sonar echoes from the shoal in 0.2s and that sound travels at 330 m/s in sea water.

Sound waves

1 Design a role play to explain how sound travels as a longitudinal wave. In your role play you may wish to include the following ideas:

- A sound wave is a wave of energy.
- Longitudinal sound waves are caused by vibrations.
- The air particles are pushed closer together, creating compressions.
- The air particles spread out, creating rarefactions.
- The sound wave transfers energy through the air.
- The air particles remain in the same position once the sound wave has passed.

Test yourself 5-6

2 **a** Which of the following statements are true and which are false?

i	Sound waves can travel through space.	**True/False**
ii	The spreading out of air particles in a sound wave is called a rarefaction.	**True/False**
iii	As the amplitude decreases, the sound will become quieter.	**True/False**
iv	Sound travels slower in solids.	**True/False**
v	Hard surfaces reflect sound better than soft surfaces.	**True/False**

b What is a compression and how is it drawn on a diagram?

c If personal headphones are used to project music into a room so that other people can listen too, the music cannot be heard clearly. Explain why this is so.

Digital 7-8

3 A businessman designed a device to deter youths from gathering in shopping areas and from 'hanging around' in places where quiet is expected at certain times of the day. Using newspaper websites (such as the *Telegraph*) as a starting point, research how this device works. Make a wiki detailing your findings and expressing your opinion about the use of such technology!

See pages 138–139 of your Pupil Book

Sounds in solids, liquids and gases

4-5

Digital

1 An experiment using a bell in a gas jar is useful when exploring how and where sound travels. Produce a PowerPoint to explain the experiment, downloading images of the equipment from the Internet and explaining the results when the vacuum pump is switched on.

Test yourself

5-6

2 An investigation is set up to determine if sound will travel through a vacuum. An electric bell is placed in a bell jar connected to a vacuum pump (Figure 2).

FIGURE 2: The bell jar experiment.

The diagrams below show different arrangements of particles.

a Before the vacuum pump is switched on, the bell can be heard. Which arrangement of particles shows how the sound travels through the air in the bell jar?

b The vacuum pump is switched on and the bell can no longer be heard. Which arrangement of particles best shows this explanation?

c Which arrangement of particles shows how the sound energy will travel through the electrical wires that support the bell?

d If the sound was travelling through a liquid, which particle arrangement would you select?

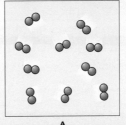
A

B

C

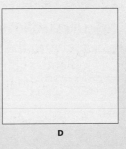
D

Creative

7-8

3 The insides of theatres and cinemas are designed to allow customers to enjoy the entertainment without echoes. However, schools can be noisy places, with sounds echoing around the building.

Imagine that you are a sound engineer – what recommendations would you make to reduce the noise levels in your school and why? Present your findings in the form of a poster to be presented to the school council.

Ultrasonic sounds

1 The chart below shows the hearing range of a number of different animals.

a i In humans the hearing range is normally between 20 Hz and 20 000 Hz. Which animals can hear above this range?

ii Which animal in the chart has the largest hearing range?

iii What is the range of hearing of the grasshopper?

b What will happen to the range of hearing of a person who works in a noisy environment?

c What precautions should workers who work in noisy environments take?

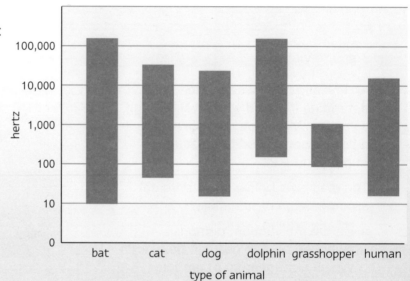

d If a dog trainer has used an ultrasonic whistle to train a sheep dog, why is it essential that he passes on the whistle to the dog handler when the dog has been trained?

2 Ultrasound has many uses; for example, it can be used to view a foetus in the womb, clean false teeth and check for defects in metal objects such as aeroplane wings. Research online the different uses of ultrasound and post your findings on a class wiki.

3 It is reported that whales could be harmed by ultrasonic sounds used in searching for oil.

In light of this, write a newspaper article expressing your opinion about whether the search for oil using ultrasonic impulses should continue. Remember, you must balance your own opinions against the needs of the country to secure oil supplies for the future.

This article on the National Geographic website is a good source of information: http://news.nationalgeographic.com/news/2006/06/060620-whales.html

The ear and hearing

1 The diagram below shows the structure of the human ear.

a Give the names for labels A–D on the diagram, selecting your answers from the following:

ear drum   semi-circular canals   auditory nerve   cochlea

b What do the ear drums do when sound waves reach them?

c What is the role of the auditory nerve?

d Which part of the ear is not related to hearing?

e You should never poke anything sharp into your ear. Explain why such an action would be dangerous and how it would affect your hearing.

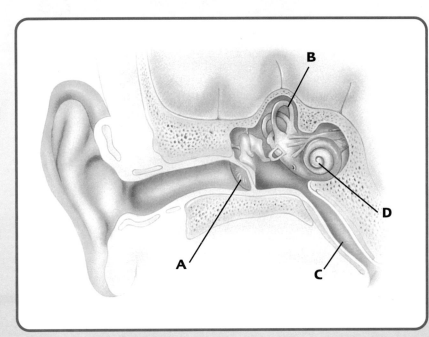

2 A hearing aid will greatly improve the quality of life for older people or people who have suffered hearing damage. Use the Internet to research how hearing aids work and why they improve hearing. Present your work as a webpage for a company manufacturing hearing aids.

3 For the parents of young children, travel sickness can be a serious problem. However, as we grow older most people grow out of getting travel sickness – except when we are in a boat in heavy seas!

a Research the symptoms and causes of travel sickness and how it can be prevented. (Hint: The NHS website is a good starting point for your research.)

b Present your work as an information leaflet that could be distributed at a doctor's surgery.

Damaging our hearing

1 a The bar chart opposite shows the estimated levels of loudness of different sounds.

    i The sound level of an MP3 player can be between 80–110 dB. Copy the chart and draw in the sound level for the MP3 player.

    ii Explain why listening to an MP3 player with the volume too high is dangerous.

  b What other sounds are also above 85 dB?

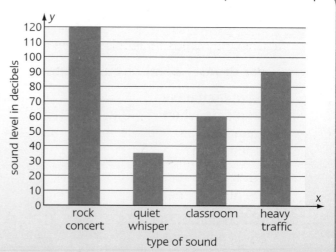

2 Your Science department is about to go on a tour in a noisy factory. Your teacher asks you to research:

- The health and safety precautions that you will encounter.
- The different ways in which you can protect your hearing on the tour.
- The hazard signs that are used in factories where there is a high level of noise.

Present your work as health and safety requirements on a company website designed for visitors and school trips to the factory.

3 Imagine that you are an airline pilot flying from the busy city airport on the map.

  a Draw out your flight plan to avoid the city centre.

  b Draw a diagram to show your rate of ascent.

  c Plan your actions for reducing engine noise.

  d Why are these actions necessary?

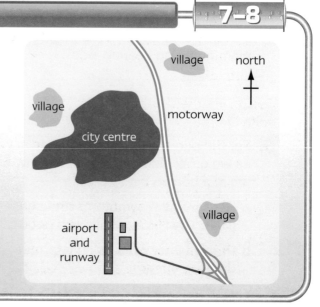

See pages 146–147 of your Pupil Book

SOUND AND HEAT PROJECT

It is cold on the way to school and your friend suggests that perhaps wearing a hat will help to keep you warm. Using the equipment listed below, you decide to plan an investigation to prove that a hat can indeed reduce heat loss from the body and is an effective way of keeping you warm on the way to school.

Equipment

- 2 250 ml beakers
- 2 thermometers
- Lids made from cork that will cover the beakers, with a central hole for a thermometer
- Kettle
- 300 ml measuring cylinder
- Stop clock

Draw a labelled diagram of the assembled equipment as you would use it.

Prediction

Use your scientific knowledge to explain your predicted results.

Plan

Now write your plan for the experiment, explaining your procedure. Give details on the following:

- independent variable
- dependent variable
- control variable
- how you will make sure your experiment is a fair test
- what you will measure
- time over which you will record the temperature
- the number of readings you will take
- potential risks to yourself or others.

Results chart

Design your results chart showing the headings and units that you will use.

Graph

Draw a sketch graph for the results you would expect to obtain. Show both sets of results on one axis. (Take care to label the axis with headings and units.)

Conclusion

Explain what you have found out by telling the story for the shape of the graph.

See pages 132–159 of your Pupil Book

Heat and temperature

4-5

Test yourself

1 **a** This kettle contains boiling water.

    i When the kettle of water is switched off, the temperature of the water will eventually cool down. Explain why.

    ii If the kettle is left for a long period of time without being switched on again, what temperature will the water cool down to? Choose from the following:

       100°C   80°C   20°C   0°C   37°C

  b Which has the most heat energy – a red hot spark from a log fire or a boiling kettle of water?

  c How do heat mats work to protect the table when a hot plate of food is placed on the mat?

  d Why are oven gloves so effective at protecting the hands when removing hot cooking pots from the oven?

Digital

5-6

2 Imagine that you are a parent and your young child is ill with a temperature. You dash to the chemist to buy a thermometer to record the body temperature of the child. The shelves display a whole range of thermometers.

  a Research the different types of thermometer used to measure body temperature to decide which type of thermometer you would select and why.
(Hint: The NHS website is a useful source of information on this topic.)

  b Explain the advantages and disadvantages of each thermometer.

  c Present your findings as they would appear on the NHS Direct website.

Creative

7-8

3 Premature babies are often placed in an incubator wearing a little cotton hat and wrapped in a silver foil survival blanket, so that their body temperature does not drop to a life-threatening level.

Produce a simple leaflet for the premature baby ward in a hospital explaining the importance of the extra clothing and foil survival blanket to small babies.

See pages 150–151 of your Pupil Book

Getting warmer

1 The police and rescue services use thermographic cameras to search for people. The camera forms images using the infra-red radiation given off by a warm body. Write an exciting story where this technology is used in a search and rescue operation. It is important to use scientific terms in your story.

2 **a** In an experiment, water was heated in a microwave oven on low and high power settings. The temperature of the water was taken before and after heating.

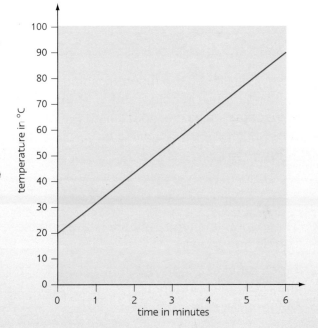

    i The graph opposite shows the temperature of the water after six minutes on a high power setting. Draw a graph to show the temperature of the water when the microwave oven is used on the lower power setting.

    ii What is the independent variable in this investigation?

    iii What is the dependent variable in this investigation?

    iv What are the control variables in this investigation?

  b Why is an infra-red lamp rather than an ordinary filament bulb used to keep new-born farm animals warm?

3 Microwaves, kettles and boilers are used in our homes to heat small quantities of water. On an industrial scale, in hot, sunny countries solar furnaces can be used for applications such as heating water.

Use the Internet to obtain a photograph of a solar furnace. Post your photograph as a wiki, with an explanation of what it is used for and how it works.

Conduction

1 Download images of **two** different kitchen appliances (for example a kettle, saucepan or toaster) from the Internet. Using these images, create a spider diagram in Word to explain why your chosen appliances are made from a combination of different materials.

2 Cold is a killer on the mountains and on the moors. It is your task to design a piece of clothing for use in cold weather. Produce an advert for your design for a Sunday newspaper magazine, explaining the materials used in manufacture and the scientific reasons for its effectiveness in keeping the wearer warm.

3 The diagrams on the right show the particle arrangement in solids, liquids and gases.

When running a bath with hot and cold water it is a good idea to test the water temperature at both ends of the bath and to stir the water before getting in.

a Why is the temperature of the bath water not uniform throughout the bath?

b Which diagram best represents the particle arrangement of the water in the bath?

c Using the particle theory, explain why it is necessary to stir the bath water.

d Which diagram would best represent the air particles in an insulator?

e If a frozen chicken is left on a stainless steel sink drainer to thaw out, which direction will the heat energy flow?

   A From the chicken to the kitchen sink drainer.

   B From the kitchen sink drainer to the chicken.

f Draw a diagram showing how the particles will behave as the chicken thaws out.

A

B

C

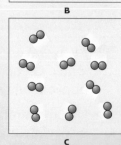

See pages 154–155 of your Pupil Book

Convection

1 Butane heaters are used to heat a small area of the garden in the chilly evening air. Environmentalists do not consider these heaters to be environmentally friendly.

   a Explain how heat energy is wasted by the butane heaters.

   b Some outside bars and cafes locate their electric heaters under a canopy. What is the role of the canopy?

   c Place the following into the correct sequence:

   A   The heating element heats the air particles

   B   The air particles begin to rise

   C   Cooler air is drawn in to replace the rising warmer air

   D   The air particles move faster

   E   The air particles expand

   F   The air particles become less dense

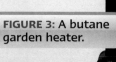

FIGURE 3: A butane garden heater.

2 Convection currents play a major role in controlling our weather and ocean currents.

   Research the importance of convection on a global scale. Present your work as a webpage for a website designed to show the links between geography and science.

3 Have you ever noticed that when you are having a picnic on the beach, the wind blows sand into your sandwich and in the evening there is a warming breeze? Convection currents are the cause of this!

   Use your knowledge about convection to draw the direction of the air movements at the beach during the day and evening.

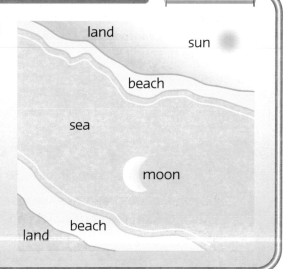

Radiation

4-5

Test yourself

1

a On a hot day which of the cars will heat up the quickest?

b The two cups contain tea at the same temperature. In which cup will the tea cool the quickest?

c Why do people who live in hot, sunny countries wear white clothing?

d Why are the handles on some pans made from black plastic?

e Ultraviolet light from the Sun gives us a suntan. The Sun also radiates heat energy as solar radiation. What unpleasant effect can this cause if we do not take precautions when sunbathing?

Creative

5-6

2 An experiment is set up as shown opposite.

When the light bulb is switched on, it will radiate heat energy.

Plot two graphs on one axis to show the predicted results for the experiment after a ten minute time period. Use your predicted plots to tell the story of the graph.

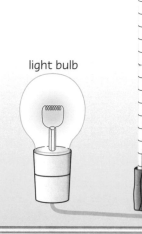

thermometer with bulb covered in silver foil

thermometer with bulb covered in black paper

light bulb

Digital

7-8

3 The vacuum flask can be used to keep drinks and food hot or cool.

Obtain a photograph of a vacuum flask from the Internet and copy it into PowerPoint. Label its features and explain how each feature keeps the food or drink contained inside hot (or cool) for a long period of time.

See pages 158–159 of your Pupil Book

Design a predator

1 The Indian Taipan is the world's most poisonous snake: one bite contains 110 mg of toxin – enough to kill up to 100 people!

Research your own amazing facts about **three** animals. The facts must be linked to the animal's adaptations. Present your work as an animal encyclopedia in the form of a wiki.

2 At the zoo, plaques on the enclosures identify the animal and give visitors information about which country it comes from, the food it eats and its life cycle.

Create your own illustrated plaque on a chosen animal, making sure that you include extra information on the animal's adaptation to its environment.

3 The common seal is an animal highly adapted for living and preying upon food in the sea.

a The body of the seal is sleek with wide, flat flippers.
Give **one** reason why such a body shape is an advantage.

b The seal is able to conserve oxygen very well when swimming.
Explain why this is an advantage.

c Beneath the fur of the seal is a thick layer of blubber.
Give **one** reason why this fat layer is useful to the seal.

d The eyes of the seal are protected by a clear membrane when diving in the sea and the whiskers on the snout are sensitive to sound vibrations in the water.
Explain why both of these adaptations are useful to the seal.

Where has the ox gone?

1 Use your knowledge of energy flow to create a complete PowerPoint called 'Energy flow through the food chain' from the diagram and text boxes below.

Where does the fruit tree gain its energy from?

Fruit tree

Hawk

Jay

The energy arrows are different thicknesses because...

2 **a** Animals use glucose as a fuel in respiration to produce energy. Copy and complete the word equation for respiration.

Glucose + ... → .... + water

b Give **one** use for the energy produced in respiration by the animal.

c Name **one** way in which some of this energy is lost from the animal.

d Why do food chains always begin with plants?

e When an animal is eaten by another animal it passes on only the food that has become part of its body and the next creature will get a smaller amount of food that has been turned into biological material. What is happening to the energy levels along the food chain?

3 Most of the world's population cannot afford to eat meat! This is a startling fact that we do not consider as we select meat from the shelves of a supermarket. Use your own knowledge to persuade your class why consuming vegetables is far more energy-efficient than rearing animals for food. Present your argument as a series of sequenced bullet points that could be used as preparation for a speech and create a pyramid of numbers to support your argument.

See pages 168–169 of your Pupil Book

Population models

1 **a i** When farmers clear areas of rainforests in order to grow crops, the animal population in the area decreases dramatically. Suggest **two** reasons why this decrease happens so quickly.

     ii Suggest why new crops grow so well in the new clearings.

     iii Explain why it is important that farmers re-plant trees when they have harvested their crops.

  b The American crayfish has invaded streams in parts of Britain. It is larger, more aggressive and eats a wider range of foods than the native crayfish. Predict what will happen to the population of the native crayfish, explaining your answer.

2 This simple food chain: lettuce ➝ rabbit ➝ fox can be used to construct the pyramid of numbers opposite.

However, the pyramid of numbers would look very different if the following changes in physical factors, biological factors and catastrophes were to take place.

Re-draw the pyramid of numbers if:

a There was a drought affecting the growth of lettuce.

b An outbreak of myxomatosis killed a large number of rabbits.

c An increase in temperature during the spring months produced a bumper crop of lettuce.

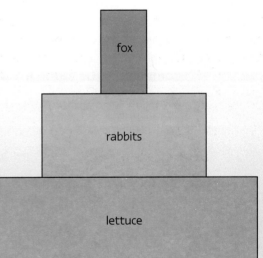

3 The fish stocks of cod in the North Sea around Britain are now dangerously low.

Launch a mock web campaign to persuade supermarkets to sell alternative fish in an attempt to save the great British fish supper of cod and chips for future generations! (Hint: Use the BBC news website to research the key facts, fish population models and possible solutions to this crisis.)

LIFE AND DEATH PROJECT

Alarmingly, the bird population in Britain is in serious decline. The number of sparrows has fallen by 90 per cent since 1970: these birds were once a common sight feeding in the garden. In the evenings, huge flocks of starlings could be seen as they flew to their roosting sites for the night, but now the wonderful flocks are a rare sight as the population of starlings has declined by 66 per cent since the mid-1970s.

The Royal Society for the Protection of Birds (RSPB) suggests that the decline in the population of wild birds may be due to the increase in intensive farming methods that are replacing traditional ways of farming.

Use your knowledge about:

- food chains
- food webs
- population models
- biological control
- pesticides

to explain your own theory behind the decline in the bird population.

FIGURE 1: Starlings.

Armed with this knowledge, you are able to help solve this problem! Design a feeding and nesting sanctuary for use on farms or on your school site. Your sanctuary must include feeding platforms and nesting boxes suitable for a number of different species of bird. It must also be secure from predators. Go on to research the type of food that you would recommend to be fed to the different birds in the different seasons.

Present your work as a fully illustrated article in a magazine called 'The Twitcher'.

The RSPB website will assist you in your project.

FIGURE 2: Intensive farming is carried out on large farms with fewer hedgerows.

FIGURE 3: Traditional farms are made up of small protected fields lined with hedges.

See pages 166–179 of your Pupil Book

Recycling by rotters

1 Foresters leave some fallen trees in a forest to rot away, rather than removing them. The fungi, microbes and insects that feed on the fallen trees play an important part in recycling.

As an enterprising garden centre owner, you decide to sell logs as a way for gardeners to introduce a natural recycling feature to their gardens. Design an eye-catching leaflet showing gardeners how your 'decomposing' product works and describing how it benefits the garden.

2 a Which of the substances below can be placed onto a compost heap?

Vegetable waste from the kitchen   **Waste food scraps**

Leaves from trees   **Biodegradable plastics**

b The labelling on lawn weed killer packaging warns not to place lawn clippings onto the compost heap for three further cuttings after applying the weed killer. Suggest **one** reason why this warning is important.

c The temperature at the centre of a compost heap can reach up to 60°C. Where does this heat energy come from?

d Compost forms layers of humus around soil particles, providing nutrients for the plants, and giving substance and structure to the soil so that it can absorb and retain water for the plants. The humus is also a source of nutrients for worms in the soil. The worms play an important part in mixing the soil and also feed on plant material that rots in the soil.

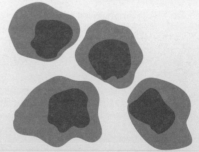

FIGURE 4: Soil particles consist of minerals surrounded by humus.

Use the information above to explain why it is important to use compost on our gardens and not simply use fertiliser to replace minerals.

e Suggest a reason why it is important to return these minerals back to the soil.

3 Disposable nappies are thought to be environmentally unfriendly. Research online and write an article for the magazine 'Mothers to Be', presenting the key information that you have found and arguing your point of view on this much-debated issue. Be sure to use scientific terms to give weight to your article.

Populations

1   **a** Complete the sentences by making a selection from each column. The statements in the centre and right-hand columns can be used more than once.

Disease		one of the animals in the food web decreases in number.
A warm spring season	increases a population because	
A drought		the number of producers in the food web increases.
A new predator	decreases a population because	
A very cold spring season		the number of producers in the food web decreases.

b In the spring, and at times when food supplies are plentiful, animals produce several offspring. Why is it important that animals do not produce just one or two offspring per year?

2   Scientists believe that climate change is responsible for changes in animal populations. Occasionally we hear of plagues of insects affecting the food chain, and even causing disease and death in some parts of the world.

a Research **one** story about a plague. The BBC news website is a good place to start your research.

b Produce your own story (using scientific terms) about a plague as a mock article for the BBC news website.

3   **a** Explain the possible reasons for the change in numbers of the chipmunk over a period of a year.

b Now imagine that you are the owl! Explain why you are hoping for good spring weather and a bumper crop of nuts and seeds.

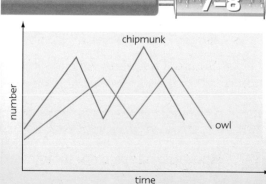

FIGURE 5: This graph shows the changes in the numbers of owls and chipmunks over time.

Biological control

4-5

Digital

1 In our supermarkets and at farmers' markets we can purchase organic produce; but what exactly is organic farming?

Research organic farming, concentrating on the methods that organic farmers use to produce their crops. (Hint: www.defra.gov.uk will help in your research.)

Use your findings to prepare material for an interview on the radio programme 'Farming Today'. Share your interview as a podcast.

Creative

5-6

2 Salmon are bred in captivity in fish farms and fed fish food pellets. Cereals used in the manufacture of these food pellets are sprayed with pesticides, resulting in small quantities of dangerous chemicals being fed to the fish. As a result of this, the Food Standards Agency has recommended that small children only be fed one portion of salmon per week.

It is hoped that when newspapers print information on such important matters, they do so without bias (without favouring a particular party). Imagine that you are a journalist working for a tabloid newspaper and the Editor asks you to write a sensationalist story about fish farming. Present your report biased in favour of either the findings of the scientists or the fish farmer.

Test yourself

7-8

3 In 1945 millions of people in India were killed by malaria spread by mosquitoes. The pesticide DDT was then used as a spray to kill the mosquito. The chart below shows the death rate in different years.

a i Suggest **one** reason why the deaths from malaria decreased between 1945 and 1960.

ii In 1960 it was discovered that DDT has a damaging effect on the environment. Why do the deaths from malaria begin to rise again after 1965?

iii Suggest why large quantities of DDT were found in the bird population.

b Drug companies are developing a vaccine against malaria. Apart from saving lives, explain why this is a positive development.

c Pesticides can be used to destroy the pest 'whitefly', but scientists are searching for a biological control of the whitefly. What is the advantage of using a biological control over the use of a pesticide spray?

Day and night

1 Select the correct choices from the words in bold to complete the sentences.

Day and night occur because the Earth **orbits the Sun/spins on its own axis**. The Earth spins at a constant speed and it takes about **one year/24 hours** to make a complete spin (or rotation). Light from the Sun falls on one half of the spinning Earth and the side facing away from the Sun experiences **day/night**. The Earth orbits the Sun once in **24 hours/28 days/365¼ days**.

2 a Your Science class visits a local primary school and the class teacher asks you to explain why the days are longer in summer and shorter in winter. You decide to draw a diagram like the one shown below to assist in your task.

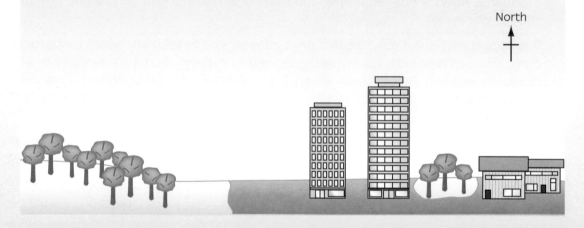

North

Draw the path of the Sun as it appears to move across the sky in the summer. Label this path with an 'S'. Now draw in the Sun's path for the winter months and label it with a 'W'.

b Explain to the class why the Sun only **appears** to move across the sky. (Be sure to include in your explanation details of when and how this idea developed.)

3 A photograph of the stars can be taken at night by pressing the shutter on a camera and leaving it open for several hours. By aiming the camera at the pole star, the stars can be tracked over this period of time.

Research photographs taken of the pole star on image sites on the Internet and use them to persuade a classmate that the Earth is indeed rotating on its axis.

The seasons

1 **a** Copy and complete the sentences below.

The seasons happen because

In winter Britain is tilted

In summer the Sun is higher in the sky and

In an Australian summer the Sun's rays hit the Earth more directly because

the Earth's axis is tilted.

the Earth orbits the Sun.

away from the Sun.

towards the Sun.

the days are shorter.

the days are longer.

the axis is tilted towards the Sun.

the axis is tilted away from the Sun.

b Imagine that you spend the summer holidays in Australia. Write a short paragraph to explain which way the Earth is tilted in the Southern hemisphere and why there will be a difference in the way the Sun is tracked across the sky in the Northern and Southern hemispheres.

FIGURE 1: Australia during the British summer.

2 Complete either activity **a** or **b**.

a Explain what it would be like to live on a planet that did not tilt on its axis.

b The Earth orbits the Sun in a slight elliptical orbit. Comets orbit the Sun in very large elliptical orbits, passing close to the Sun and then travelling great distances into space. What would it be like to live on a planet with such an elliptical orbit?

Present your work as a diary of changes in the weather over the period of one year.

3 Imagine that you live in northern Finland! Use the Internet to research the problems of living in the very far reaches of the Northern hemisphere. Describe the day length and the problems encountered by the plants and animals that live in these harsh conditions. Present your work as an illustrated fact sheet for the Christmas tourists.

The Moon

1 Research the story of the first Moon landing. Write the TV script for this momentous event, reporting to the world the achievements of Neil Armstrong and Buzz Aldrin.

2 Figure 2 shows the positions of the Sun and the Earth.

The Moon is a satellite of Earth, and in the same way as the Sun appears to move across the sky, the Moon appears to change in appearance throughout the month.

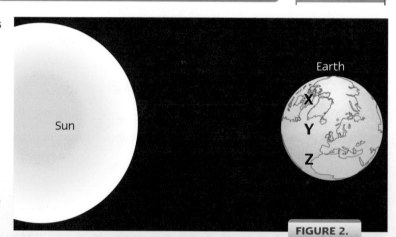

FIGURE 2.

a Draw in the position of the Moon on a sketch of Figure 2 so that an eclipse will occur at **point X**. Label it **A**.

b Draw in the position of the Moon on a sketch of Figure 2 to show a lunar eclipse. Label it **B**.

c Figure 3 shows observations of a solar eclipse from points **X**, **Y** and **Z** on Earth. Using your answer from part **a**, match the observations to locations.

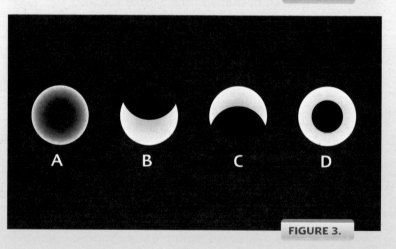

FIGURE 3.

3 **a** Research the names and shapes given to the different phases of the Moon for one lunar month, also showing the phases for the next week ahead. Present your findings (including images) in an article explaining the phases of the Moon for the journal '*Astronomy Weekly*'.

b If possible, check the phases that you have researched in reality by viewing the Moon at night.

The Solar System

Test yourself 4–5

1 **a** Link the words to their correct definitions.

Planet	A rocky planet.
Pluto	A gaseous planet.
Moon	Shape of pathway followed by the planets when orbiting the Sun.
Jupiter	A satellite of the Sun that reflects light.
Sun	Closest planet to the Sun.
Ellipse	No longer classified as a planet.
Mercury	Nuclear reaction in its core generates heat and light energy.
Mars	Orbits the Earth once every 28 days.

b Place the following in order of size, starting with the smallest object.

Planet **Universe** **Star** **Moon** **Solar System** **Galaxy**

Creative 5–6

2 Complete an alphabet challenge based upon the words used in the topic of Space. A couple of examples have been completed for you, but see if you can think of different words.

Remember, you must find words for all 26 letters of the alphabet, but if in difficulty you may extend the rules (as shown with letter 'D'.)

A – Asteroid; B – ? ; C – ? ; D – Dark side (of the Moon)

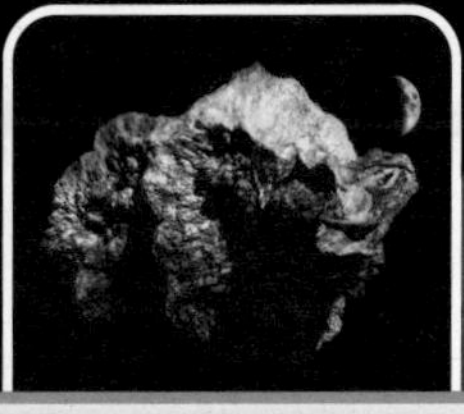

FIGURE 4: Asteroids are minor planets.

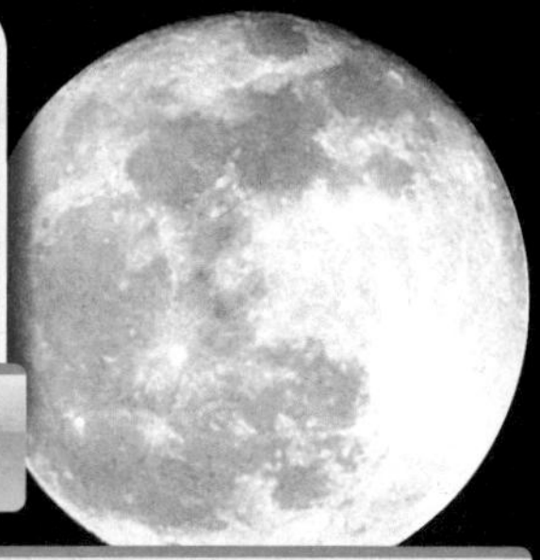

FIGURE 5: The Moon is a natural satellite of the Earth.

Digital 7–8

3 Research the planets online.

a i Use the information that you find to make a set of fact cards on the planets.

ii Colour code your fact cards into rocky and gaseous planets.

iii Organise the planets into patterns according to information on the distance from the Sun and time taken to orbit the Sun.

iv Use your fact cards to test your classmates' knowledge of the Solar System.

b Bring together all the facts that you have gathered and present them in an imaginative way for a website such as www.sciencemonster.com/planets.html.

See pages 192–193 of your Pupil Book

Gravity in space

4-5

Creative

1 Gravity holds the planets in orbit and pulls us to the surface of the Earth.

If we travel downwards very quickly in a lift or on a very fast roller coaster, we can feel weightless – almost as though gravity has disappeared. Imagine life without gravity. Write an account highlighting the advantages and disadvantages of life without gravity.

5-6

Test yourself

2 **a** Copy and complete the sentences by selecting from the words shown below:

> **smaller**   **rotation**   **further away**   **orbit**
> **gravitational field**   **speed**   **closer**   **larger**

Gravitational force is responsible for keeping the planets in .... around the Sun. The Moon is in orbit around the Earth due to the .... mass of the Earth. The .... objects are, the greater the gravitational force. The planets stay in orbit around the Sun because of their .... and the .... of the Sun.

b What would happen to the Earth if the Sun's gravitational field was to decrease?

7-8

Digital

3 Your class is given the following statement:

'Once in orbit around the Earth, artificial TV satellites will remain there without a power source.'

Use the Internet to research the power systems used by satellites.

Present the findings from your research in the form of a diagram and use it to argue against this statement and to persuade the rest of your class why these power systems are necessary, even though gravity helps to keep the satellite in orbit.

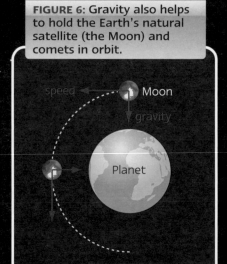

FIGURE 6: Gravity also helps to hold the Earth's natural satellite (the Moon) and comets in orbit.

speed   Moon
gravity
Planet

SPACE PROJECT

Imagine that you are Space Director at Mission Control NASA. Your brief is to plan the next mission to Mars. There are a large number of factors to consider.

Suggested strategy:

1 You must consider the objectives of the mission: what scientific investigations will you complete, what data will you collect and what experiments will you carry out?

2 Research the planet – what gases are present, what is the temperature, how long is a day and a year?

3 Research the journey time and how long the mission would remain on Mars.

4 Explore how your astronauts will survive in space – an inhospitable environment where astronauts will be exposed to harmful radiation and cosmic rays for extensive periods of time.

5 You could also consider:

- the problems of zero-gravity on the journey
- a design for a space suit
- surviving the journey (looking at food resources, oxygen supplies and even coping with potential illness).

Your role:

You may wish to concentrate upon **one** aspect of the mission:

- Making a model of the launch rocket, space suit or Mars robot vehicle.
- Producing a wall chart based on the facts about Mars.
- Designing experiments to be carried out when you reach Mars.
- Taking on the role of Quarter Master – organising the supplies for the mission and planning survival strategies on the journey (such as growing high-energy crops using energy from the sunlight).
- Planning the journey by looking at the forces involved and the challenges of living in zero-gravity.

Hint: www.spaceflight.nasa.gov/mars is a good starting point for your research.

See pages 186–205 of your Pupil Book

Gravity and weight

Creative   4–5

1 Astronauts living on a space station on the Moon have run out of sugar for their tea!

Produce a poster for a classroom display showing the mass and weight of a 1kg bag of sugar on the Earth, in space and when you arrive on the Moon in your space shuttle.

Test yourself   5–6

2 **a** Copy out the diagram opposite. On your diagram, draw force arrows to show the direction of gravity acting on the astronauts standing on the surface of the Moon.

b When the astronauts are on the surface of the Moon, which of these effects will they observe?

They will be able to jump higher than on Earth.

They will be weightless.

They will be able to hit a golf ball further than on Earth.

Their mass will be less than it is on Earth.

c You hear this conversation in a supermarket between a customer and a shop attendant:

"I can only find flour sold in 500g bags. I would like to buy a bag of flour with a weight of 1kg."

Use the correct terms to re-write the conversation.

d Your friend weighs himself on a set of Newton scales and finds that he weighs 400N. What will your friend's **mass** be?

Digital   7–8

3 Look at the table on page 199 of the Pupil Book. It shows data that astronomers have collected on the rocky planets. Complete the following activities:

a Produce a line graph of the data using Excel.

b i Use your graph to determine the trends in the data.

ii Using the trends that you have identified, describe the advantages and disadvantages of living on each planet compared to Earth.

c i Add to your graph data on a new planet, Planet X, situated beyond Mars.

ii Use this data to produce a wiki entry describing what life is like on Planet X.

Satellites

1 Artificial satellites play a major role in our everyday lives, orbiting the Earth and transmitting, among other things, TV signals, weather pictures and telephone signals back to Earth.

Design a simple satellite action computer game or board game. Make sure that you cover all of the different uses for artificial satellites and that your game is challenging and fun!

(Hint: Your design must be imaginative and exciting – to get you started, here is a potential design for a board game.)

Play your game with a classmate next lesson.

electrical storm closes down TV satellite – go back 3 places

Discovered new moon – move on 2 places

3,2,1 launch satellite

orbit successful

2 **a** Sketch out the diagram of the Earth below.

   i Add to the diagram the orbit of a TV satellite above the Earth.

   ii Draw the signal from the satellite to a TV dish on a house on Earth.

   iii Why is it important that the satellite remains in a fixed orbit above the Earth's surface?

   b Why do the following people rely on satellites?

   i weather forecasters

   ii intelligence services

   iii astronomers.

   c Add to your diagram the Earth's natural satellite and label the name of this natural satellite.

3 Conduct research online into the orbits of geostationary and polar orbiting satellites. Produce a diagram of the satellites to explain how they work, describe their current uses and mention any potential uses that they could have in the future. Post your findings as a wiki.

Space travel

1 **a** On the graph opposite name the two missing planets, **X** and **Y**.

b Why will space travel to Jupiter and beyond be a difficult challenge?

c If man did manage to travel to another planet, what difficulties would they find in surviving?

d Earth is becoming over-populated, and fossil fuels are increasingly difficult to source and unable to meet the needs of the population. Is it realistic for us to be looking for another planet to live on in our galaxy? Explain your reasons.

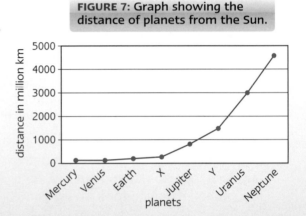

FIGURE 7: Graph showing the distance of planets from the Sun.

2 Many young children would like the opportunity to become astronauts when they grow up! Design an application form to test prospective candidates who wish to fulfil their lifetime dream. Your questions should be based on **ten** facts about the Solar System and space, and must include questions about the need for and challenges of space travel (you could consider time problems and problems relating to survival in space).

3 Research on the NASA website:

a The speed that rockets have to go to escape the Earth's gravitational field on a space mission.

b The orbit speed of satellites providing TV signals for our homes.

On Earth we have maximum speed signs for travelling on our roads. Present your research as a minimum speed sign for astronauts! Use cartoon images from the Internet to make your sign imaginative and informative.

FIGURE 8: A spacecraft needs to overcome Earth's gravity to be launched into space.

See pages 202–203 of your Pupil Book

Exploring further

Digital 4–5

1 Visit the NASA website and research **one** of the following:

- the International Space Station
- the Space Shuttle
- famous space probes
- future missions into space
- space suits and how they work
- exciting discoveries.

Gather your facts as a mock NASA webpage and use it to inform your class on your chosen subject next lesson.

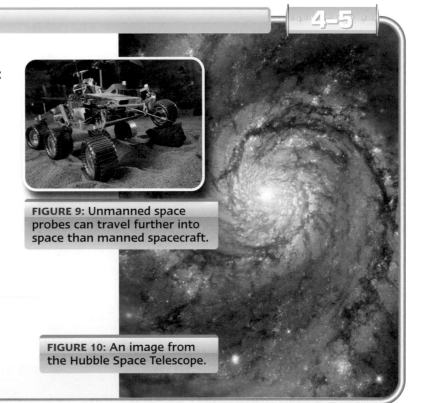

FIGURE 9: Unmanned space probes can travel further into space than manned spacecraft.

FIGURE 10: An image from the Hubble Space Telescope.

Test yourself 5–6

2 **a** Scientists have observed the planets and stars for hundreds of years using telescopes. Give **two** advantages of launching a telescope located on a satellite.

b A 'Space Station' orbits the Earth and is manned by astronauts and scientists as part of the International Space Mission. Why is the mission valuable to mankind's understanding of space?

c What was the advantage to be gained from launching the Hubble Space Telescope into space when we have powerful telescopes on Earth?

d What is the advantage of sending an unmanned space probe to a planet over using a telescope?

Creative 7–8

3 Your task is to design your own unmanned space probe to carry out research on the surface of Mars.

Present your design as a magazine feature or an illustrated journal article. Be sure to include information on the experiments it would carry out and to draw in the equipment that it would need to carry.

MAGNETISM PROJECT

Article 1: The government plans for more energy from wind farms

The Prime Minister is pressing ahead with the policy of generating more electricity from sustainable energy sources in an attempt to reduce carbon dioxide emissions by 60 per cent by 2050.

As part of the energy policy, Britain is committed to obtaining 15 per cent of its energy from renewable energy sources by 2020.

The government believes that Britain has the best wind resources in Europe, and is planning to construct 7000 more wind turbines. The government reports that wind farms cut carbon emissions, therefore reducing our dependency upon fossil fuels.

In a public report, the government revealed that up to 80 per cent of the population is in favour of wind power and that 64 per cent would be happy to live within 5 km of a wind farm.

The environmental groups Greenpeace and Friends of the Earth see wind farms as an opportunity to tackle climate change and reduce the need to import fuels from abroad as well as creating jobs in the construction industry.

MAGNETISM PROJECT

Article 2: Wind power is too unreliable to produce electricity for our future needs

A recent report has found that wind turbines will fail to meet the electricity needs of the country at times of peak demand. The report also states that electricity from wind power is expensive and fossil fuelled power stations will need to be on standby when the wind is not blowing with sufficient speed to turn the turbine blades.

Wind farms cannot operate at full capacity because of the unreliable nature of the wind in Britain. Indeed, evidence shows that in the winter months of January and February, wind farm efficiency can drop to four per cent of its maximum output when energy from the wind is insufficient to generate the electricity demanded. As a result, carbon savings will be less than expected because fossil fuel power stations are still needed as a back up during periods when the wind is calm.

Even if wind power can be used as a renewable energy source, the Renewable Energy Foundation is concerned that subsidies given to wind farm construction are an expensive way of reducing greenhouse emissions. In addition, they may be expensive to maintain because at high wind speeds there is an added risk of the blades of the turbine being damaged.

Offshore wind farms have the added disadvantage of difficult construction and high maintenance costs due to high corrosion caused by the salt spray in the wind. Added to this is the fact that wind farms may kill birds of prey.

Wind farms constructed too close to houses also have an effect upon property prices due to noise pollution and an obvious visual impact. Due to this, campaigners for the Protection of Rural England are also concerned about the rapid growth in wind farm construction.

Acknowledgements

The Publishers gratefully acknowledge the following for permission to reproduce copyright material. Whilst every effort has been made to trace the copyright holders, in cases where this has been unsuccessful or if any have inadvertently been overlooked, the Publishers will be pleased to make the necessary arrangements at the first opportunity.

The Publishers would like to thank the following for permission to reproduce photographs:

p. 6 © iStockphoto.com / Kelly Cline; p. 7 © iStockphoto.com / Hannamariah photography, © The Print Collector / Alamy; p. 10 © iStockphoto.com / Hannamariah photography, © Tarzoun – Fotolia.com; p. 13 © Sheila Terry / Science Photo Library; p. 14 © 2008 Jupiterimages Corporation; p. 15 © iStockphoto.com / Ken Brown, © James King-Holmes / Science Photo Library; p. 16 © Eraxion. Image from BigStockPhoto.com; p. 17 © National Cancer Institute / Science Photo Library; p. 18 © iStockphoto.com / dra_schwartz; p. 19 © iStockphoto.com / sgame, © iStockphoto.com / © Carolina K. Smith, M.D., © Roger Harris / Science Photo Library, © iStockphoto.com / © Abel Leão; p. 20 © iStockphoto.com / © Carolina K. Smith, M.D.; p. 22 © iStockphoto.com / Andreas Reh; p. 25 © Jeff Gynane – Fotolia.com; p. 26 © iStockphoto.com / Lisa Thornberq; p. 28 © Amorphis – Fotolia.com; p. 31 © Seen – Fotolia.com, © Ruslan Olinchuk – Fotolia.com, © Ruslan Olinchuk – Fotolia.com; p.32 © Ruslan Olinchuk – Fotolia.com; p. 33 © Adam Bies – Fotolia.com, © Charles D. Winters / Science Photo Library; p. 34 © iStockphoto.com / gwmullis; p. 36 © Shariff Che'Lah – Fotolia.com, © Ackley Road Photos – Fotolia.com, © iStockphoto.com / inkastudio, © Tan Kian Khoon – Fotolia.com, © iStockphoto.com / Gerville, © Eray Haciosmanoglu – Fotolia.com, © iStockphoto.com / leezsnow, © Dario Sabljak – Fotolia.com, © Douglas Freer – Fotolia.com; p. 38 © DTKindler. Image from BigStockPhoto.com; p. 41 © iStockphoto.com / Jan Kranendonk; p. 42 © Inventavision. Image from BigStockPhoto.com; p. 48 © iStockphoto.com / Tore Johannesen; p. 49 © Paul Gibbings. Image from BigStockPhoto.com; p. 50 © GOL – Fotolia.com; p. 52 © US Department Of Energy / Science Photo Library; p. 53 © Vinicius Tupinamba – Fotolia.com; p. 56 © iStockphoto.com / ericsphotography; p. 57 courtesy of the author; p. 59 © M. Dauenheimer, Custom Medical Stock Photo / Science Photo Library; p. 61 © Jason Stitt – Fotolia.com, courtesy of Mike Cryer; p. 64 © Kirsty Pargeter – Fotolia.com; p. 65 © MargoJH. Image from BigStockPhoto.com; p. 66 © fckncg. Image from BigStockPhoto.com; p. 66 © Michael Shake. Image from BigStockPhoto.com, © matka_Wariatka. Image from BigStockPhoto.com; p67 © LR Scott – Fotolia.com; p. 68 © Jawslk – Fotolia.com, © Steve mc. Image from BigStockPhoto.com, © iStockphoto.com / Andrew Howe; 70 © Vedmochka. Image from BigStockPhoto.com, © Gudellaphoto – Fotolia.com, © WeeCat. Image from BigStockPhoto.com; p. 72 © Gail Johnson. Image from BigStockPhoto.com, © PhotoMan – Fotolia.com; 75 © Robert Harding Picture Library Ltd / Alamy; 77 © Lynne Williamson – Fotolia.com, © tdoes – Fotolia.com; 78 © Leona Barratt; 79 © Florent DIE – Fotolia.com, © NASA Kennedy Space Center (NASA-KSC), © NASA Jet Propulsion Laboratory (NASA-JPL); p. 82 © NASA Marshall Space Flight Center (NASA-MSFC); p. 83 © Jim Sugar / Corbis, © NASA Goddard Space Flight Center (NASA-GSFC)

Name: ....

Organisms, Behaviour and Health	4-5	5-6	7-8
Keeping Healthy			
A balanced diet			
Is my diet OK?			
Eating food			
Do I have enough energy?			
A breath of fresh air			
A healthy heart			
Measuring your pulse			
How do you know if you are fit?			
Studying Disease			
History of disease			
The infection cycle			
Preventing disease			
Sexually transmitted diseases			
Biological warfare			
Vaccination			
What are vaccines?			
How to get rid of microbes			
Are microbes useful?			

Chemical and Material Behaviour	4-5	5-6	7-8
Separating Mixtures			
Dissolving rocks			
Sweet tooth			
Pure salt			
Super solvents			
Distillation			
Better boiling			
Drinking water			
Chromatography			
Atoms, Elements and Compounds			
Chemical alphabet			
Getting sorted			
All mixed up			
What are compounds?			
Understanding equations			
Combining elements			

Name: ....

Energy, Electricity and Forces	4-5	5-6	7-8
Magnetism			
Magnetic materials			
Magnetic fields			
Earth's magnetic field			
Explaining magnetism			
Electromagnetism			
Using electromagnets			
Motors and generators			
Power stations			
Burning problems			
Renewable energy resources			
What about nuclear power?			
Sound and Heat			
What is sound?			
Describing sounds			
Speed of sound			
Sound waves			
Sounds in solids, liquids and gases			
Ultrasonic sounds			
The ear and hearing			
Damaging our hearing			
Heat and temperature			
Getting warmer			
Conduction			
Convection			
Radiation			

The Environment, Earth and Universe	4-5	5-6	7-8
Life and Death			
Design a predator			
Where has the ox gone?			
Population models			
Recycling by rotters			
Populations			
Biological control			
Space			
Day and night			
The seasons			
The Moon			
The Solar System			
Gravity in space			
Gravity and weight			
Satellites			
Space travel			
Exploring further			

Topic 1 – Keeping Healthy

A balanced diet

a Carbohydrate

b Cheese spread

c Protein

d So that nutritional information between different foods can be compared easily.

e 5%

Is my diet OK?

a Vitamins and minerals can reduce the risk of cancers.

Too much salt can be responsible for increasing blood pressure.

Fish oils rich in omega-3 can reduce the risk of heart disease.

Too much carbohydrate can be responsible for obesity.

Too little fibre in the diet can be responsible for bowel cancer.

Too much salt can be responsible for swelling of the feet.

b The kidney

c More energy is used by the body during exercise, therefore 'fuel' consumption must be increased during training.

d 18 hours

e After 18 hours without a main meal your body will be very short of energy stores and your blood sugar levels will be very low, making you tired and completely lacking in energy.

f Oily fish are rich in omega-3 fatty acids that help to keep the heart healthy as well as providing important nutrition for the brain.

Eating food

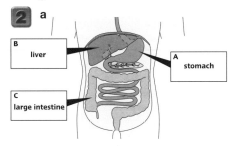
a

b Label D located on or pointing to the small intestine.

c Large molecules of starch, protein and fats cannot be absorbed into the blood. Digestion breaks down the size of the molecules so that they can be absorbed into the blood.

d Enzymes

Do I have enough energy?

a Food supplies your body with **energy**. This energy is used in the body for movement, **growth**, repair and to keep us **warm**.

oxygen + glucose ➞ **carbon dioxide** + water + **energy** used for movement

b Energy from our food is used by the body to keep us warm. We therefore need to eat more in the cold months of winter so that we can stay warmer.

c The school children of today may need less energy than children needed a generation ago because many do not walk or cycle to school and many spend their spare time indoors (on computers or watching TV) rather than taking part in sport or strenuous activities.

d The increase in obesity among young children indicates that many consume too much food, and that too much of this food is fatty and high-calorie/energy. Many young children also fail to take part in strenuous exercise and do not burn off the excess calories/energy.

A breath of fresh air

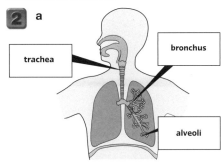
a

b Diffusion

c One from: large surface area; moist; thin cell walls.

d Breathing is the physical process of inhaling and exhaling air.

Respiration is the production of energy in the cells of the body.

e Mucus from the mucus-producing cells traps the dust particles and the cilia on the ciliated cells sweep the mucus and dust up and out of the lungs.

A healthy heart

a Fatty food causes damage to the coronary artery.

Lack of exercise can lead to obesity.

Carbon monoxide reduces the availability of oxygen in the blood.

Nicotine causes addiction to smoking.

Tar causes cancer.

b

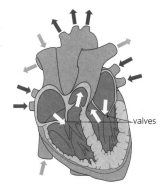

—valves

Measuring your pulse

a i 68 bpm

ii Increasing the activity from resting to running increases the pulse rate.

iii The pulse rate readings would be higher.

b A – Airway; B – Breathing; C – Circulation

How do you know if you are fit?

a Sara needs a balanced diet; water; fibre.

b Your pulse rate and breathing rate will increase.

c Oxygen and sugars

d In the muscles

Topic 2 – Studying Disease

History of disease

a Louis Pasteur – Demonstrated that life was not created from rotting meat.

John Snow – Demonstrated that disease could be spread by contaminated water.

Robert Koch – Demonstrated that anthrax was spread by spores.

Edward Jenner – Demonstrated the first vaccination.

b i Scientific studies reveal a trend: more people that smoked contracted lung cancer than people who did not smoke.

ii Studies showed the following trend: more people who lived in a smoky atmosphere contracted lung cancer than people who did not.

The infection cycle

a Bacteria reproduce through cell division.

b Doctors can prescribe antibiotics to treat a bacterial infection.

c A new strain of the bacteria may develop resistance to the prescribed antibiotic and is therefore more difficult to treat. A different antibiotic may be needed for successful treatment.

d Antibiotics cannot be prescribed to treat a viral infection.

Preventing disease

a Microbes

b i

 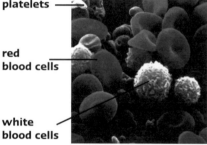

platelets —

red blood cells

white blood cells

ii White blood cells.

iii Platelets

c i Two days

ii The antibiotics destroyed the infection.

iii Five days

iv To ensure that the infection is completely destroyed.

Sexually transmitted diseases

a i Wearing gloves

ii To prevent contamination

b There is a chance that their latest sexual partner has also become infected and so they must be tested.

c AIDS

Biological warfare

a A steady increase in the number of infections until the sixth day when the increase becomes more rapid.

b The workers should be isolated and quarantined.

c Redraw as a steeper curve on the graph.

d Redraw with the graph levelling off and then rate of infection falling.

e Students to give own argument with clear reasons.

Vaccination

a Immune means 'will not catch the disease'.

b White blood cells

c There has been a recent increase in cases of measles and it is important that children are vaccinated to reduce the number of cases.

d Redraw to show a gradual fall in the rate of increase of the disease.

e Vaccination of the population in the isolated area before it could spread to the wider public.

What are vaccines?

a White blood cells – Produce antibodies to attack the infection.

Antibiotics – Medicines used to treat bacterial infection.

Antitoxins – Produced by white blood cells.

Platelets – Responsible for forming a scab to seal a wound in the skin.

Toxins – Poisons produced by microbes.

Vaccine – Weakened form of the disease introduced into the body.

b The newborn baby can receive antibodies from the mother's breast milk. Antibodies will also have entered the baby's system from the mother's blood before birth.

c When travelling abroad, the country may have diseases that we have not been vaccinated against. As a result we may contract these diseases and become ill (and even possibly die, depending on the disease). You could also spread the diseases to this country upon your return from holiday.

How to get rid of microbes

a B

b The cream has destroyed the fungal infection at A and C.

c C

d i The diameter of the clear area around the disc soaked in the cream.

ii The disc soaked in distilled water.

e Viruses can only live inside living cells – it could not live on the jelly.

f The bacteria mutate when they reproduce and become immune to the antibiotics. Therefore it is necessary to develop new ones.

Are microbes useful?

a 20°C

b 37°C

c 120°C

d 4°C

e −4°C

f −18°C

Topic 3 – Separating Mixtures

Dissolving rocks

a B – Limestone

b Burning the fossil fuels coal and oil.

c calcium carbonate + sulphuric acid → calcium sulphate ($CaSO_4$) + carbon dioxide (CO_2) + water (H_2O)

Sweet tooth

a i The solubility of potassium nitrate and lead nitrate increases with temperature. The solubility of sodium chloride is the same at all temperatures.

ii Balance or scales

iii Temperature

iv Amount or mass of solute added

b Increase the temperature of the water.

c The salt will again dissolve until the water is saturated. Increasing the temperature will again increase the solubility of the water.

Pure salt

a A solid that dissolves in a **solvent** to form a solution is called a **solute**.

b Evaporation

c Wear eye protection; if heating, take care with Bunsen burner and turn it off when evaporation is complete.

Super solvents

a Salt is insoluble in alcohol.

b The solution was saturated.

c Increase the temperature or volume of the water.

Distillation

a Boiling

b To condense the steam into water.

c 100°C

d (Liebig) condenser

e The alcohol in perfume has a lower boiling point than salt water.

f The alcohol in the perfume is flammable.

Better boiling

 a A water jacket was added to cool and condense the hot vapour effectively.

b i The ice is melting.

ii The water is heating up.

iii Draw the line on the graph increasing slightly more and then levelling off.

iv Plot a point at 100°C.

Drinking water

 a A – Distillation; B – Filtration; C – Evaporation

b i Evaporation (C)

ii Distillation (A)

iii Filtration (B)

c i Desalination

ii The seawater is boiled to remove the salt. The steam is condensed as drinking water.

Chromatography

 a Blue

b Alcohol

c The ink from pen 2 (brown).

d The ink from a pen would separate and make the chromatography results confusing/incorrect.

Topic 4 – Atoms, Elements and Compounds

Chemical alphabet

 a

Element	Symbol	Element	Symbol
Carbon	C	Gold	Au
Magnesium	Mg	Iron	Fe
Copper	Cu	Chlorine	Cl

Element	Symbol
Silver	Ag
Calcium	Ca
Oxygen	O

b Students' own examples

c There are 6 atoms of carbon, 12 atoms of hydrogen; 6 atoms of oxygen. This means there is a total of 24 atoms in a molecule of glucose.

Getting sorted

 a Copper in an electrical wire – Good conductor of electricity.

Aluminium in a saucepan – Good conductor of heat.

Gold in jewellery – Does not react with oxygen.

Iron in a compass needle – Magnetic.

b Inert gas (hydrogen)   D

Non-metals   C

Metals   B

Very reactive metals   A

Inert gases   D

c Na is likely to have similar properties.

All mixed up

 a Elements: chlorine, nitrogen, copper

Compounds: sodium chloride, rust, glucose, carbon dioxide

Mixtures: sea water

b i Any two from: mixtures can be separated; mixtures have the properties of the component parts; mixtures can be made from different proportions of different components; there is no chemical change in a mixture.

ii A new substance is formed with different properties from iron and sulphur.

iii The air is cooled until it is a liquid. The gases are then separated by boiling.

What are compounds?

 a i A ii B iii D iv E v C

b When two or more **atoms** join together, a **compound** is formed. Iron **oxide** is a **compound** formed from iron and oxygen, and iron sulphide is a compound formed from iron and **sulphur**.

Understanding equations

 a Oxygen

b magnesium + oxygen ➡ magnesium oxide

c i More

ii The magnesium has gained the element oxygen and will therefore increase in mass.

Combining elements

 a sulphur + oxygen ➡ sulphur dioxide

b i Sulphur

ii Oxygen

c

d $H_2 + O \rightarrow H_2O$

e Water

Topic 5 – Magnetism

Magnetic materials

 a If the metal was magnetic it would be repelled by the magnet.

b i N–S

ii Aluminium is not magnetic (or it cannot be magnetised).

iii One from: iron, nickel, steel.

Magnetic fields

 a The magnetic field

b N–S

c N ➡ S

Earth's magnetic field

 a S pole located at the top; N pole located at the bottom

b From N ➡ S

c Geographic North pole is at the axis of the Earth's rotation (at magnetic South pole).

Explaining magnetism

 a Redraw with all aligned ⬅

b At the ends (the poles).

c X = South pole, Y = North pole

Electromagnetism

 a Adjusting (any two from): the number of turns of insulating wire; the current; the number of cells in the battery.

b By counting the number of paperclips in the chain that are attracted to the magnet.

c Steel retains its magnetism.

d Soft iron

e The paperclips would not be attracted.

Using electromagnets

 a i The number of turns of wire on the soft iron bar.

ii The mass of iron filings picked up by the electromagnet.

iii One from: electric current; number of cells in the battery.

b The strength of an electromagnet can be controlled and electromagnets can be turned on and off.

c A large current will flow through the live wire, increasing the strength of the electromagnetism and attracting the iron contact and switching off the mains current.

d Steel retains its magnetism and does not release the magnetic material when the electromagnet is switched off.

Motors and generators

 Stage A – Starting to cycle slowly or starting to cycle up a hill.

Stage B – Increasing in speed or cycling down a hill.

Stage C – Cycling at a steady, quick speed.

Stage D – Slowing down rapidly.

Stage E – Stopped or waiting at a road junction or traffic lights.

Power stations

 A – Fuel supply

B – Furnace

C – Boiler

D – Steam

E – Turbine

F – Generator

G – Condensor

Burning problems

 a Coal, gas or oil

b sulphur + **oxygen** → sulphur dioxide

c The production of sulphur leads to acid rain.

d Fossil fuel + **oxygen** → carbon dioxide + **water** + energy

e The production of carbon dioxide leads to global warming.

Renewable energy resources

 a Coal, gas

b Hydroelectric, wind, tidal

c Geothermal

d Gravitational potential energy → kinetic energy → electrical energy

e Bio-fuel will remove carbon dioxide during photosynthesis but then release carbon dioxide when the fuel is burnt.

What about nuclear power?

 a Nuclear radiation can cause cancer and death.

b The nuclear reactor producing heat energy replaces the furnace.

c Nuclear power stations do not give off the carbon dioxide that is associated with global warming.

d De-commissioning is the controlled closing down of the nuclear power station and protection of the station for many years due to the nuclear radiation.

Topic 6 – Sound and Heat

What is sound?

 a Sound can't travel through a vacuum because there is no atmosphere and therefore no air particles to vibrate.

b i Pluck the string harder.

ii The longer the string, the lower the pitch. The shorter the string, the higher the pitch.

iii The thick string will have a lower pitch and the thin string a higher pitch when plucked.

iv The tighter the string, the higher the pitch.

Describing sounds

 a D

b B

c 'A' has a longer wavelength than 'B'.

d Draw in the distance from the middle of the wave to the maximum peak or trough height.

e

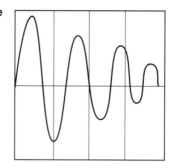

f When we are speaking there are constant changes in pitch and amplitude.

Speed of sound

 a Sound and light energy

b Light travels quicker than sound.

c The energy level decreases as the sound energy spreads out and is dissipated.

d In solids

e Light can travel through the vacuum of space.

Sound waves

 a i F **ii** T **iii** T **iv** F **v** T

b A compression is a region of the sound wave where the air particles are squashed together producing a high-pressure region. A compression is drawn as compressed lines close together.

c Sound energy from the ear speakers is insufficient to travel any great distance.

Sounds in solids, liquids and gases

 a A

b D

c C

d B

Ultrasonic sounds

 a i Bat, cat, dog and dolphin

ii Bat

iii Approximately 90–1100 Hz

b There will be a decrease in their upper frequency range.

c They should wear ear defenders or ear plugs.

d The dog will only respond to the commands from the ultrasonic whistle.

The ear and hearing

 a A – Ear drum

B – Semi-circular canals

C – Auditory nerve

D – Cochlea

b Vibrate

c To transmit nerve impulses to the brain.

d Semi-circular canals

e It would be dangerous because it may burst the ear drum causing pain and severely damaging the hearing.

Damaging our hearing

 a i Bar drawn up to 80 dB and then extended to 110 dB.

ii Above 85 dB the level of sound could damage the hearing permanently. If someone else can hear your MP3 player when you are wearing headphones, the level of sound is too high and damage may be caused to your hearing.

b Rock concert; heavy traffic

Heat and temperature

 a i Heat energy will be lost and dissipated to the surrounding environment.

    ii 20°C

b Boiling kettle of water

c The mat is made from an insulating material and prevents the conduction of heat through to the table.

d The gloves are manufactured from an insulating material and air gaps between the layers of material insulate the hands from the hot cooking pot.

Getting warmer

a i Draw a graph with the same starting temperature, a less steep gradient and a lower end temperature.

    ii The power settings on the microwave oven

    iii The temperature of the water

    iv The volume of water, time and starting temperature of the water

b The infra-red lamp is safer and will not burn the skin if touched for a short time.

Conduction

a Water is a poor conductor of heat energy.

b B

c The water molecules are not packed together and therefore the vibrations will not be passed on rapidly, resulting in different temperatures of water in different parts of the bath. It is necessary to stir the water to ensure uniformity of temperature.

d C

e B – From the kitchen sink drainer to the chicken.

f Draw a diagram showing the particles vibrating more as the chicken begins to thaw out.

Convection

a Through convection – although conduction and radiation are also responsible for heat energy wastage.

b The canopy reduces heat loss by reducing convection currents.

c A, D, E, F, B, C

Radiation

a The black car will heat up the quickest.

b The tea in the black cup will cool down the quickest.

c The white clothing reflects the heat energy and keeps the wearer cooler.

d The black handle is a good radiator of heat energy.

e Sunburn

Topic 7 – Life and Death

Design a predator

a The streamlined body shape reduces friction/drag, increasing swimming speed.

b It enables the seal to dive deeper when hunting for fish without frequently returning to the surface for air.

c It is useful (one from): as insulation against the cold water; for buoyancy; as a high-energy store.

d The clear membrane allows the seal to see prey under water. The whiskers allow the seal to detect the vibrations created by prey that it is unable to see.

Where has the ox gone?

a Glucose + **oxygen** ⟶ **carbon dioxide** + water

b Heat or movement

c One from: faeces, urine, heat energy, breathing out, movement

d Plants gain their energy from the Sun through photosynthesis and thus are located at the beginning of the food chain.

e The energy levels in the food chain are decreasing.

Population models

a i Loss of habitat, therefore fewer places to live, breed and shelter; loss of food supply.

    ii There is more light for photosynthesis; more space for growth of new plants; increase in nutrients for new plant growth.

    iii To return the habitat to its original state and for the animal population to increase.

b The population of native crayfish will decrease because it cannot compete for food and space needed to breed.

Recycling by rotters

a Vegetable waste from the kitchen; leaves from trees

b Chemicals in the lawn clippings will remain in the compost and will kill the plants when the compost is used on the garden.

c Energy from microbial respiration

d The compost replaces nutrients, gives structure, absorbs and retains water for the plants, and is food for the worms that play an important role in the soil. These things cannot come from fertiliser alone.

e To replace nutrients removed by plants growing in the garden.

Populations

a Disease decreases a population because one of the animals in the food web decreases in number.

    A warm spring season increases a population because the number of producers in the food web increases.

    A drought decreases a population because the number of producers in the food web decreases.

    A new predator decreases a population because one of the animals in the food web decreases in number.

    A very cold spring season decreases a population because the number of producers in the food web decreases.

b The animal must produce more than one or two offspring because not all of them will survive and without over-population the species may die out in that area or even become extinct.

Biological control

a i DDT was used to kill mosquitoes, therefore reducing the deaths from malaria.

    ii DDT stopped being sprayed and this allowed the increase in the population of the mosquito, causing an increase in deaths from malaria.

    iii The birds feed on lots of insects found in the food chain and DDT increases up the food chain.

b It may result in fewer applications of pesticides.

c Chemicals in the pesticide spray will enter the food chain and may accumulate and eventually poison the top predator. A biological control is therefore preferable to the use of chemicals.

Topic 8 – Space

Day and Night

 Day and night occur because the Earth **spins on its own axis**. The Earth spins at a constant speed and it takes about **24 hours** to make a complete spin (or rotation). Light from the Sun falls on one half of the spinning Earth and the side facing away from the Sun experiences **night**. The Earth orbits the Sun once in **365¼ days**.

The seasons

 a The seasons happen because the Earth's axis is tilted.

In winter Britain is tilted away from the Sun.

In summer the Sun is higher in the sky and the days are longer.

In an Australian summer the Sun's rays hit the Earth more directly because the axis is tilted towards the Sun.

b In the British summer months the Northern hemisphere will tilt towards the Sun and the Sun will be high in the sky. The opposite is therefore true of the Southern hemisphere during these months, leading to more wintery weather.

The Moon

 a

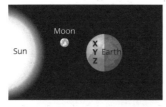

b

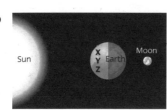

c X – C
Y – A
Z – B

The Solar System

 a Planet – A satellite of the Sun that reflects light.

Pluto – No longer classified as a planet.

Moon – Orbits the Earth once every 28 days.

Jupiter – A gaseous planet

Sun – Nuclear reaction in its core generates heat and light energy.

Ellipse – Shape of pathway followed by the planets when orbiting the Sun.

Mercury – Closest planet to the Sun.

Mars – A rocky planet.

b Moon, Planet, Star, Solar System, Galaxy, Universe

Gravity in space

 a Gravitational force is responsible for keeping the planets in **orbit** around the Sun. The Moon is in orbit around the Earth due to the **larger** mass of the Earth. The **closer** objects are, the greater the gravitational force. The planets stay in orbit around the Sun because of their **speed** and the **gravitational field** of the Sun.

b Earth would begin to escape from the Sun's gravitational field and disappear into space.

Gravity and weight

 a Draw force arrows acting downwards towards the centre of the Moon.

b They will be able to jump higher than on Earth.

They will be able to hit a golf ball further than on Earth.

c "I can only find flour sold in 500g bags. I would like to buy a bag of flour with a **mass** of 1kg."

d 40kg.

Satellites

 a i

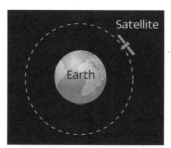

ii

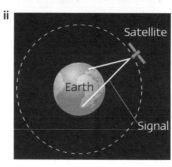

iii TV satellite dishes would need to move to track the satellite across the sky if the satellite did not remain in a fixed orbit. In a fixed orbit, satellite dishes point directly at the TV satellite.

b i Weather forecasters – to take photographs of weather systems.

ii Intelligence services – spying and gathering intelligence (such as the position of military bases).

iii Astronomers – to take photographs of deep space.

c

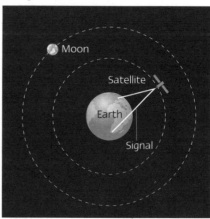

Space travel

 a X – Mars, Y – Saturn

b Distance from Earth is realistically too far to travel.

c Lack of resources – food, water and oxygen supplies would not be available; it would be too cold due to greater distance from the Sun; amount of time it will take to travel beyond Jupiter and the impact of this on the spacecraft.

d Students to give own answer with explanation.

Exploring further

 a Two from: can see deeper into space; less distortion from atmosphere so can obtain clear images; more information gathered.

b The International Space Mission allows scientists to study the effect of space travel on the human body, to test and develop new materials, and to make observations of the Earth (including studying weather patterns and the effects of climate change).

c The images will be much clearer and the Hubble Space Telescope is able to view deeper into space as it moves further away from the earth.

d The unmanned probe can gather information on the conditions on the planet and take samples for analysis, sending the data back to Earth. There is also not the problem of how astronauts will survive on the journey to consider.